COURAGEOUS
Dreaming

Also by Alberto Villoldo, Ph.D.

Dance of the Four Winds (with Erik Jendresen)

The First Story Ever Told (with Erik Jendresen)

The Four Insights*

Healing States (with Stanley Krippner, Ph.D.)

Island of the Sun (with Erik Jendresen)

Mending the Past and Healing the Future with Soul Retrieval*

Millennium Glimpses into the 21st Century

The Realms of Healing (with Stanley Krippner, Ph.D.)

Shaman, Healer, Sage

Yoga, Power, and Spirit*

≈ ≈ ≈

*Available from Hay House

Please visit Hay House USA: **www.hayhouse.com**®
Hay House Australia: **www.hayhouse.com.au**
Hay House UK: **www.hayhouse.co.uk**
Hay House South Africa: **www.hayhouse.co.za**
Hay House India: **www.hayhouse.co.in**

COURAGEOUS
Dreaming

HOW

SHAMANS

DREAM

THE WORLD

INTO BEING

ALBERTO VILLOLDO, PH.D.

HAY HOUSE, INC.
Carlsbad, California • New York City
London • Sydney • Johannesburg
Vancouver • New Delhi

Published and distributed in the United States by: Hay House, Inc.: www.hayhouse.
com • *Published and distributed in Australia by:* Hay House Australia Pty. Ltd.: www.
hayhouse.com.au • *Published and distributed in the United Kingdom by:* Hay House
UK, Ltd.: www.hayhouse.co.uk • *Published and distributed in the Republic of South
Africa by:* Hay House SA (Pty), Ltd.: www.hayhouse.co.za • *Distributed in Canada by:*
Raincoast Books: www.raincoast.com • *Published in India by:* Hay House Publishers
India: www.hayhouse.co.in

Editorial supervision: Jill Kramer • *Design:* Amy Gingery

Library of Congress Cataloging-in-Publication Data

Villoldo, Alberto.
  Courageous dreaming : how shamans dream the world into being / Alberto Villoldo.
-- 1st ed.
      p. cm.
  ISBN 978-1-4019-1756-2 (hardcover) -- ISBN 978-1-4019-1757-9 (tradepaper) 1.
Shamanism--South America. I. Title.
    BF1622.S63V53 2008
    299.8--dc22
                                        2007034823

Hardcover ISBN: 978-1-4019-1756-2
Tradepaper ISBN: 978-1-4019-1757-9

1st edition, March 2008

Printed in the United States of America

CONTENTS

Courageous Dreaming

We are what we think.
All that we are arises with our thoughts.
With our thoughts, we make the world.
— BUDDHA

Whether we realize it or not, we are all dreaming the world into being. What we're engaging in is not the sleeping act we're so familiar with, but rather a type of dreaming we do with our eyes open. When we're unaware that we share the power to co-create reality with the universe itself, that power slips away from us, causing our dream to become a nightmare. We begin to feel we're the victims of an unknown and frightening creation that we're unable to influence, and events seem to control and trap us. The only way to end this dreadful reality is to awaken to the fact that it too is a dream—and then recognize our ability to write a better story, one that the universe will work with us to manifest.

The nature of the cosmos is such that whatever vision you have about yourself and the world will become reality. As soon as you awaken to the power you have, you begin to flex the muscles of your courage. Then you can dream bravely: letting go of your limiting beliefs and pushing past your fears. You can start to come up with a truly original dream that germinates in your soul and bears fruit in your life.

Courageous dreaming allows you to create from the source, the quantum soup of the universe where everything exists in a latent or potential state. Physicists understand that in the quantum world nothing is "real" until it is observed. The distinct packets of energy known as "quanta" (which consist of particles of matter as well as light) are neither "here" nor "there"; in a sense, they are everywhere in space/time until you or I decide to take note of them. When we do so, we tease them out of the web of infinite possibilities and collapse them into an event in time and space. These energy quanta like to link up with each other once they've selected a particular form of manifestation. As soon as they manifest, reality becomes fixed: Our reality is "here" instead of possibly everywhere.

But quantum events do not occur in the laboratory only. They also happen inside our brain, on this page, and everywhere around us. Even if they're separated by millions of miles, or by days or weeks, these quanta of energy remain intimately linked; consequently, if you interact with one, you affect the entire system that this energy is part of. When you access any part of the dream, the great matrix of creation, you can change reality and alter the entire dream, and its effects will ripple to the past and influence the future.

Modern physics is describing what the ancient wisdom keepers of the Americas have long known. These shamans, known as "the Earthkeepers," say that we're dreaming the world into being through the very act of witnessing it. Scientists believe that we're only able to do this in the very small subatomic world. Shamans understand that we also dream the larger world that we experience with our senses.

Like the Australian Aborigines, the Earthkeepers live in an environment where the dreamtime has not been pushed into the domain of sleep like it has for the rest of us. They know that all of creation arises from, and returns to, this creative matrix. The dreamtime infuses all matter and energy, connecting every creature, every rock, every star, and every ray of light or bit of cosmic dust. The power to dream, then, is the power to participate in creation itself. Dreaming reality is not only an ability but a duty, one all humans must perform with grace so that our grandchildren will inherit a world where they can live in peace and abundance.

We've actually already gone into extraordinary detail to dream our universe into being. Immediately after the big bang, 99.99 percent of all matter and antimatter in the cosmos went on to annihilate each other. The stars and galaxies that we see around us today are all that remained, a minute portion of what once was. Had the ratio of matter to space in the universe changed by even one-billionth of a percent, the laws of physics that permit life to emerge would not have been possible. The big bang had to be so perfectly orchestrated and calculated that it produced only one part of matter in 10 to the 50th power of stardust. This is divided by 10 followed by 50 zeroes, no more and no less. That this occurred purely by chance is possible only if we contemplate the existence of a very large number of universes in the cosmos, where an improbable event such as the creation of our own universe would have been plausible!

What's even more baffling is the fine-tuning of the parameters of the universe that occurred on the surface of the earth, which has maintained a perfect temperature balance between the freezing and boiling points of water for more than a billion years. The unlikeliness of these ratios that permit life to appear suggests the presence of an intelligent force, not a creator or a god but a universe power, which the Earthkeepers call "the dreamtime" or "infinity."

The Earthkeepers I have studied with in the Andes and the Amazon believe that we can only access the power of this force by raising our level of consciousness. When we do, we become aware that we're like a drop of water in a vast, divine ocean, distinct yet immersed in something much larger than ourselves. It's only when we experience our connection to infinity that we're able to dream powerfully. In fact, it's our sense of separation from infinity that traps us in a nightmare in the first place. If this sounds like circular thinking, you're right. Which came first, the nightmare or the sense of separation from infinity? The answer is that they occur simultaneously.

To end the nightmare—to reclaim your power of dreaming reality and craft something better—you need more than the recognition of how this process works. You need to have a visceral understanding of your dreaming power and experience it in every cell of your body. The intellectual comprehension of your ability to create reality mimics but then forestalls the kind of dreaming you're capable of. If you don't get beyond mere intellectual comprehension of this concept, you'll end up lowering the bar and creating a far less glorious and beautiful experience of the world than what you're capable of crafting. With a visceral understanding of your power to dream, you realize that you can share this experience of infinity right here, right now, and stop feeling dissociated and disconnected.

It takes courage to taste infinity. According to Greek mythology, the gods swiftly punished any mortal who dared to ascend Mount Olympus and taste divine power. Yet they ultimately rewarded those who had the courage to step into their realm, such as Hercules and Psyche. Similarly, in Judeo-Christian lore, as soon as Adam and Eve disobeyed God and ate of the fruit of the tree of knowledge of good and evil, making human beings more like God, He threw them out of the Garden of Eden, "lest [humankind] put forth [their] hand, and take also of the tree of life, and eat, and live for ever" (Gen. 3:22). But despite this original sin of humanity, all men and women are promised a chance to dwell in heaven at the end of time.

Once you experience dreaming, you realize that everything in your life is unfolding with perfect synchronicity. Events may not be working out the way you'd like them to, but within the greater scheme of things, they *are* happening in superlative harmony. For example, you miss the train to work on the day that terrorists strike the World Trade Center and survive (which actually happened to a student of mine). Or your child tells you that he's been accepted to the college of his choice the same week you get the promotion you've been hoping for. If the universe seems to be conspiring against you, on the other hand, then you need to change the dream.

With courageous dreaming, you discover that your problems are no longer overwhelming you or defining your life. While the difficulties you face feel very real, you always have the choice to create a heroic account about your relationship to them instead of a disempowering saga of suffering. You'll recognize that you can stop being a victim, trying to fix the world all on your own, or feeling vindictive toward those who harmed you. You'll see that your life is exactly as it should be right now, and you'll be able to let go of all the stories that keep you feeling trapped and unhappy and venting in your therapist's office. You'll begin to practice dreaming the world into being, and everything will change.

The Earthkeepers believe that the world is real, but only because we've dreamed it into being. But dreaming requires an act of courage, for when we lack it, we have to settle for the world that's being created by our culture or by our genes—we feel we have to settle for the nightmare. To dream courageously, we must be willing to use our hearts. Otherwise, our dreams will stall at the level of thinking, planning, and worrying too much. Then our dream will turn into a nightmare or mere fantasy, trapping us or drifting away while we wonder, *What happened?*

~ ~ ~

I remember one of my early trips to the Amazon. I was then a young anthropologist investigating the healing practices of the shamans of the rain forest, and I'd decided to use myself as a subject. I explained to the jungle medicine man that as a child I'd fled my country of birth because of a communist revolution. I had seen bloodshed in the streets and been terrified by gunfire in the night. Since then I'd suffered from recurring nightmares in which armed men would force their way into my home and take away my loved ones. At the time I was in my late 20s, yet I'd been unable to enter into a lasting relationship for fear that I'd lose the person I loved, just like in my nightmare.

During one healing ceremony, the shaman explained to me that like everyone, I can either have what I want or the reasons why I can't. "You are too enamored of your story," the old man said. "Until you dare to dream a different dream, all you will have is the nightmare."

That evening I learned how I could craft a different story for myself, one in which I'd been tempered by adversity and my experiences had taught me to have compassion for others who were suffering. The first step to dream my new dream was to create a new story in which I wasn't playing the part of the victim. I then realized that not only was I dreaming my life, but I was also dreaming the entire cosmos into being, just as it was doing with me.

Although the mind resists it, the fact is that like me, you have a choice between having the life you want or the reasons why you can't. You can luxuriate in joy and peace, or you can continually be burdened by that big black bag full of all the sorrowful incidents and accidents that happened to you in your childhood or last relationship. You can endure your wounds or you can enjoy your glory. You can live the life of a victim, burdened by the traumas of your past, or you can live the life of a hero, but you can't do both. If you want to feel empowered, you need to make a conscious decision to create a sacred dream and practice courage.

Courageous dreaming happens at a state of perception that the Earthkeepers refer to as the level of *hummingbird*. The hummingbird is an archetype for the heroic voyager—just like it, you'll inevitably take some wrong turns. However, each time you return to the recognition that you are dreaming your reality, you will deepen your understanding of the journey and feel more committed to it. You'll be able to embrace the ever-shifting landscape around you with equanimity and a sense of humor, and you'll even experience grace.

Recognizing That You're Living in a Nightmare

The word *dreaming* conjures up the strange sequence of images that unfold in our minds when we're asleep. Dreams can also be metaphors: We aspire to achieve the American dream, a dream house, a dream romance, or a dream career. We look at the problems in our world and say we dream of an end to poverty, violence, and global warming; what we mean is that we believe we're indulging in wishful thinking, describing what we feel can never really come true. Yet neither our sleeping creations nor wishful thinking is the kind of dreaming we'll be exploring in this book.

If you're like most people, your original plan for the "dream life" went awry somewhere. You examined what went wrong, tinkered with the plan, put aside the disappointment, and tried again . . . and still failed. You may be at a point where you're beginning to lose faith that you can have a fulfilling and meaningful existence, or you might feel powerless to create the destiny you want. Maybe you got distracted and forgot what you'd originally envisioned, and now you feel that you're only going through the motions of existence, unsure of your purpose. "Dreaming" may seem frustrating and futile.

When we become caught up in the activities of everyday survival, as well as trying to fashion a life that our mind tells us ought to make us happy, we can become confused. The relationship sours, the carefree lifestyle vanishes, and the bills pile up—or we look around at all the symbols of success that we've acquired and wonder why they don't make us happy. Our formula for bliss turns out to be a recipe for banality at best and suffering at worst, and our dream becomes a nightmare.

Much as we like to think of ourselves as leading bold and original lives, we tend to lose our zest for adventure at an early age as we begin conforming to our culture's expectations of how we ought to think, feel, and act. We've been educated into a cultural nightmare that promotes apathy instead of courage and conformity instead of originality. We don't feel a sense of fulfillment or purpose, but we dare not admit that our lives aren't working for us. It can be so scary to even think about paying the consequences for going up against the status quo that we just stay right where we are, afraid to rock the boat.

Such was the case when I was at San Francisco State University. At that time I was one of the youngest clinical professors in the state-university system, and I also directed my own lab, the Biological Self-Regulation Laboratory. One day it occurred to me that perhaps I was looking out of the wrong end of the microscope, that instead of going smaller and smaller to understand the mind, I had to go bigger, to the point that I considered a paradigm whose rules about time and space were vastly different from the one I'd been trained in. That was when I heard a faint call to leave the lab and travel to the Amazon, where I could study the shamans who relied entirely on the power of the mind to create what I was then calling "psychosomatic health."

All of my friends thought I was mad, that I was throwing away a promising career for a wild adventure in the jungle. The only one happy to see me go was the dean, who believed that all consciousness research was a waste of time and money. I remember how ashamed I felt, and how disappointed my family was, that I was leaving a "respectable" job at the university and becoming an explorer. (Even many years later, when I was in my 40s and had authored half a dozen books and lectured at universities worldwide, my mother asked me when I was going to "get a real job" at a university—a position that she felt was prestigious in contrast to the work I was doing.)

Recalling how we've been shamed in the past for being different makes us so uncomfortable that we project that shame onto each other and subscribe to a collective nightmare of powerlessness and fear. We're suspicious of anyone who thinks, feels, and acts differently from everyone else, and we're secretly jealous of them, too. Caught up in this nightmare, we stop taking risks and become cynical. Our trust in others erodes, and we insist that we can look out for ourselves without help from anyone.

We'd like to believe that we're living our lives creatively, that we're iconoclastic and fascinating, but we come up with mundane rebellions such as driving a flashy red car rather then a neutral-colored one or wearing a Hawaiian shirt to work instead of a suit. Unfortunately, our creative acts have become empty symbols, and life has become a parody of a television soap opera, with people playing stereotyped roles and acting out tired old scripts.

Lack of originality and courage are the hallmarks of our collective nightmare. Since all of us have a fundamental need for the sense of security that familiarity provides, we long to fit in and take comfort in believing that tomorrow will be just like today. In fact, psychologist Abraham Maslow, who identified a hierarchy of human needs, found that men and women place the need for security above the one for love. Change causes us to face the unknown and reside in the realm of unfamiliarity, so we avoid it. Before taking a step out the door, we want plenty of reassurance that we won't experience any discomfort and that our path will be clear at all times and lead us straight to our goal. Any uncertainty is enough to make us close the door completely. It seems less painful to stick with what's familiar, even if we're continually grumbling and complaining about how awful it is.

Admitting that what we're doing isn't producing the results we'd like takes courage. While I was at my lab at the university, I could have continued receiving research grants to perform studies that I knew wouldn't be significant. I'd tried to convince myself that since I was getting funding from respected foundations, I was doing something that made a difference. When I decided to travel to the Amazon, not one of my sponsors was willing to back my work, and the only colleague who supported me was my professor, Dr. Stanley Krippner. Once I realized that I'd been lying to myself about the importance of my academic career, I had to let go of my pattern of responding to my discomfort by doing the same thing I'd always done—only with a surge of recommitment. I had to stop hoping that if I tried hard enough, I'd find a way to do work that had some meaning and still have the blessing of a major university.

The United States has always embraced the metaphor of being born again to passion and commitment. American bookstores are filled with memoirs about athletes and movie stars who kicked their drug habits, poor men and women who became extraordinarily wealthy, and fat and unhappy people who transformed themselves into thin and happy people. But no matter how much enthusiasm we have for reinvention, unless we let go of the dreams and wishful thinking that got us into the nightmare in the first place, we'll keep re-creating it in some form or another. We think we're being reborn, but before long we discover that we're still rolling the boulder up the hill like Sisyphus, getting nowhere. The ex who drove us crazy is gone, but our new partner is just as exasperating; or that career change we'd been praying for landed us in yet another job dominated by office politics. No wonder we feel powerless! We want world peace, or at least peace in our lives, but we can't have a conversation with our former romantic partner or current co-worker without becoming furious.

You *can* stop engaging in futile efforts and feeling stuck in a nightmare, but to do so, you must make a radical shift in how you perceive reality. No self-help course will help you with this, and understanding what you ought to do isn't enough. You have to reclaim your power to dream boldly and courageously, conscious of your journey through infinity. Only then can you easily and naturally let go of the fear that keeps you bogged down in your personal nightmares.

Dreaming a Life of Purpose and Meaning

While we've been told that creating material security will make us feel good, even those who achieve success according to our culture's standards are often shocked by how empty their triumphs are. Some of my clients are multimillionaires whose wealth most people would envy, but many don't enjoy any sense of purpose or happiness at all. All some of them can think about is how awful it would be if they were to lose what they've accumulated, which is often the reason they come to see me in the first place. They want to heal from the curse placed on them by society—the mandate to attain and accumulate. They want to discover how to have a life rich with meaning and purpose instead.

Other clients who haven't reached their goals tend to focus on the future, saying, "I'm going to change my life and make the world a better place, just as soon as my kids are grown/I fully fund my retirement plan/I get a less stressful job." They're waiting for all their distractions to move out of the way so that they can take advantage of their big chance to prove how bold and original they can be. But in the present, they're in the middle of a collective nightmare that's uninspired, unoriginal, and unsustainable . . . one that's making them feel as if they are slowly dying.

Many of us are like the frog stuck in a pot of water that's slowly boiling. In this oft-told story, the creature feels the water growing increasingly warmer, but instead of saying to himself, "I'd better jump out before it gets too hot and I really suffer," he keeps adjusting to the temperature. Eventually, the poor thing is boiled to death. Right now, the water is beginning to simmer around us—we need to stop hoping that things will get better someday and just *jump.*

All too often, in our panic we reach for a quick fix that requires minimal effort, and we talk ourselves into believing that we've found a shortcut to happiness. We send our child to a new school, thinking that will solve all the problems she was having at the old one, only to find that she's just as unhappy as she was before.

On a collective level, we scramble for the same types of solutions: In the past several years, Ecuador has lost 40 percent of its rain forests due to drilling for oil to feed the insatiable American appetite for fossil fuels. Yet they only ended up harvesting enough oil to fuel the United States for two weeks. It's clear that quick fixes can be painfully expensive and futile, and they land us right back in that pot of boiling water—we still have the same problems of limited fossil fuels, economies dependent on them, and global warming.

One reason why we scramble to find fast solutions instead of accessing our courage and dreaming something new is because we falsely believe that courage requires sacrifice. Yet it's actually cowardice that requires the greatest sacrifice: that of our convictions, principles, dreams, and hopes. Panicking and trying to create material security never works for long, and the cost is very high. Giving up what we most value causes much worse suffering than relinquishing someone else's approval or some of our own material comfort. It's far better to forget about quick fixes and learn to access the courage to dream.

The Courage of the Soul

The word *courage* derives from the Latin word *cor,* meaning the heart or soul. Courage of the soul goes beyond mere bravery. When we're brave, we take risks in order to meet our survival needs. The tales of military heroes who fight to the end despite the enemy's overwhelming numbers are extraordinary, but they're driven by the urge to survive. With the courage of the soul, we don't focus only on self-preservation, security, or safety; in fact, such courage compels us to risk our comfort and safety, and sometimes even our lives, as we act according to our most deeply held values. This kind of valor comes from a higher source and is the necessary ingredient for us to create a different dream.

Your dream may be one of peace or adventure, parenting or teaching, nurturing or healing. And although a dream is not formulated in words but is steeped in vision, instinct, and feelings (much like your sleeping dreams are), it can be described in words. Here are a few examples: "I want to fully savor the life I have and enjoy my children being present at work when I'm in the office and present with my family when I'm home," or "I want to live adventurously, exploring my options and listening to my heart," or "I want to make a difference in the world in whatever way Spirit guides me." Unlike longings, hopes, or even concrete goals, these affirmations can manifest in every moment when you hold them in your heart. Then you naturally and easily behave in accordance with your dream, accessing the tremendous power of courage.

When you're dreaming courageously, you're experiencing a higher level of awareness and caring, but you're not blissed-out like a monk on a mountaintop, nor are you stuck merely trying to survive. You're present in your experience, not focused on the past or the future. So if you're bagging up the recycling to take to the curb, for instance, you're simultaneously aware that you're participating in the care and nurturing of the planet. If you're waiting in line to get your driver's license, you accept being told that you didn't fill out the form properly; you don't start writing a story in your mind about your hellish afternoon dealing with bureaucracy.

Said another way, you recognize your connection to others and perceive that you aren't the only one who matters, and you genuinely care about the good of all of Earth's creatures. You care about the clerk behind the window and the nervous teenager waiting to take his behind-the-wheel test. You recognize that your fear doesn't justify inflicting it on anyone else and your frustration doesn't justify taking it out on anyone else.

Courage of the soul takes us beyond petty human emotions and lets us live authentically, speaking our truth and breaking the rules even when it's embarrassing or uncomfortable to do so. It allows us to take a stand in the small moments instead of waiting for our grand-slam opportunity to prove our mettle, our "Rosa Parks moment of greatness."

Actually, not even Rosa Parks herself waited for her moment of greatness. By the time she refused to give up her seat on a Montgomery, Alabama, bus to a white person in 1955, she'd already been involved in the struggle for civil rights for years, and she'd been an NAACP secretary and youth leader of the local branch. She'd stood up to bus drivers before but had never been arrested for her actions. She was already living according to her values and supporting others who were living according to theirs. She remained seated, breaking the law, not because she was particularly tired that day or because she suddenly and serendipitously found a wellspring of courage that had been hidden until that magic moment—she simply lived her life in alignment with her deepest values and purpose, so when she needed courage, it was there for her. Acting out of integrity did not take enormous effort or willpower, for it was her established habit.

Until the day Mrs. Parks died, she maintained that she was uncomfortable with being credited with starting the Montgomery bus boycott. She understood that it just as easily could have been started by another person who, like she, was living a life of integrity and courage, and who would have done the same thing she had under the circumstances. Yet this story has been rewritten to feature a brave iconoclast who instantaneously accessed a vein of courage that had been buried until that key moment, thus launching a revolution—as if the real story wasn't inspiring enough.

Waiting for your grand Rosa Parks moment is disempowering because it keeps you from developing the habit of living courageously in each small moment. Like Mrs. Parks, however, you can develop the habit of *dreaming* courageously, of choosing to create a new and better reality right now instead of waiting for your life to get better. This book and the exercises herein will help you access the strength to act, to clean up the mess in the river of your life, and to stop reliving and retelling the same stories of victimhood and powerlessness.

You can decide to risk your comfort rather than deny your most deeply held principles. You can be honest with yourself and others, love without fear, and heal yourself and your relationships. You can stop hiding from the painful truth that you aren't always living up to your ideals. You can laugh at yourself, find beauty in any moment or situation, and become the changes you'd like to see in the world. Then you can achieve the goal of being ready to die at any instant—an attitude that allows you to stop being afraid and instead appreciate life and the precious time you have to experience it.

Once you're no longer trapped in the nightmare, you can begin the process of dreaming and watch as the universe mirrors back the change in yourself by altering the circumstances around you. But while you'll no longer need to make a Herculean effort to try to create happiness and fulfillment in your life, you will have to say yes to every opportunity for living courageously. The moment you find yourself beginning to tell a lie to protect your ego, scripting a story of victimhood, or giving up your proverbial seat on the bus and muttering "Well, maybe next time," you need to awaken to your power to dream and let a surging stream of soul courage rush in.

When you dream courageously, the effects aren't always immediately visible in the physical world. The most dramatic changes will occur inside of you, quietly, as you make the choice to reject the unreasonable expectations of your culture, family, neighborhood, and church; let go of the need to be accepted, liked, or admired; and admit that you may feel unsafe, insecure, or unsuccessful. You draw upon the courage of the soul when you choose to look at things differently and create a different type of life for yourself. When you do that, the circumstances of your immediate environment will begin to transform.

None of us will ever reach a permanent state of enlightenment and be able to take off our shoes, put up our feet, and know for certain that we're free of all our issues and at peace with our situation at all times. Inevitably, the very moment we begin to feel that way, the universe will provide us with the perfect opportunity to realize how ridiculous and arrogant we're being. For this reason, we must make a start toward dreaming the world we say we want to exist in and the lives we say we want to lead. First we have to recognize just how paralyzing it is to live in the nightmare we've scripted for ourselves, as well as how we've colluded in the cultural nightmare that we share. Let's turn the page and begin.

PART I

From Nightmare
to Dream

CHAPTER ONE

Escaping the Nightmare

*I believe in looking reality
straight in the eye and denying it.*
— GARRISON KEILLOR

When I was 15, I was deeply infatuated with a girl who was on the local swim team with me. Rose was the most beautiful young woman I'd ever met, and my heart ached whenever I was in the water with her. I was far too timid and shy to tell her how I felt, even though I often swam next to her and experienced sheer pleasure each time a small ripple washed over me from her lane. As we did our laps side by side, separated only by the floating lane marker, my imagination took flight. I saw us declaring our undying love for each other, and I envisioned her tears of joy as I dropped to my knee and asked her to marry me. I imagined her smile as I came home from work to our little cottage on a hillside, our laughing children running toward me with open arms.

I was completely caught up in this dream, which never came true for Rose and me. A far more confident boy on our team wooed her, and they ultimately wed. I kept the secret of my infatuation hidden inside me as Rose and I went off in different directions. Eventually, I married another woman, assuming that my life would unfold according to the fantasy that had played in my head like a movie, with this woman taking over Rose's role of adoring wife and mother.

To my great shock, I discovered that my dream marriage soon became a nightmare. My wife wasn't happy raising our children while I worked, and my job at that time was unfulfilling and draining. The little cottage on the hillside ended up being a run-down townhouse in a noisy and dangerous neighborhood on the wrong side of San Francisco. I felt powerless and trapped; the more I tried to make my life work according to what I'd previously envisioned, the more I suffered. After many years and the failure of that marriage, I realized that I'd been living in a nightmare fabricated by my culture, community, and family. I'd never questioned its value or imagined that I might create something different for myself.

Many people today are in a similar situation, although they might not know it. You may even be one of them, pulled along into a linear progression—from school to marriage, career, parenthood, and middle age—without questioning whether this path is the right one for you and what your purpose is. In a corner of your consciousness, a faint voice whispers, "There must be more to life than this," but you're afraid to acknowledge its message. Lacking the courage to admit that you're a co-conspirator in a nightmare that isn't making you feel empowered or happy, you simply choose to avoid thinking about the discomfort. You continue plodding forward, one foot in front of the other.

To quench our thirst for meaning and help us escape from the nightmare, we often seek power, fame, influence, authority, or money, hoping that if we have enough of these things, then perhaps the dream might work for us. We may reach for a quick fix, acting impulsively or repressing our difficult feelings with a bottle of wine, an extramarital affair, or a flurry of activity that keeps us so busy we simply don't have time to think, feel, or dream. We don't realize that we have the power to wake up from the nightmare and open our eyes to a new day—and that we can do so without changing the spouse, the job, or the children.

Overcoming Apathy

We could end the nightmare at any time because we have all the recipes for success and happiness we need. Unfortunately, we rarely use them. This reminds me of the recent visit I paid to a friend of mine who's trapped in a desperate marriage and by a schedule that's killing him. He's 40 pounds overweight and realizes that he needs to exercise more and meditate, but has no time for either. His diet is terrible, although he knows that he really should be eating better. The irony of it all is that my friend's bookshelves are lined with self-help volumes . . . many of which he's authored!

As we sipped a glass of wine, he began to tell me of his woes. "Why don't you take some of your own advice?" I replied.

"I don't have the time or the money," he confessed.

This man had fallen into apathy. His belief in his powerlessness was keeping him stuck, unable to change anything in his life. Apathy manifests as depression and "learned helplessness"—the belief that all of one's past experiences are evidence of the utter futility of trying to affect one's life. People who suffer from learned helplessness think they have no control over their situations, so even if their suffering is great, they won't take the smallest action to change matters because they figure, *What's the point?*

My friend cared enough about his life to take a hard look at it and admit that it wasn't working, but for all the solutions he was aware of, he couldn't muster the effort to implement them. He simply didn't have the courage to act. I shared with him what the old shaman had said to me in the jungle, that we can either have what we want or the reasons why we can't. My fellow author kept choosing the reasons why he can't: "I don't have the time or the money."

When we throw cold water on every opportunity life offers us for fixing a situation, we exhaust ourselves and everyone around us. When we're apathetic, we have an endless string of excuses for why we can't act. The people who love and want to support us burn out and avoid us because they can't stand hearing yet another reason for why we have no power to change our lives.

Apathy is the opposite of courage. It makes us so cowardly that we float through our lives like ghosts, disconnected from any sort of purpose or passion. We fret about all that's wrong in the world and in our lives, but we can't recognize that we could make a difference. We don't find the courage to change, and we don't bother looking for it either.

When we live without courage, we create a nightmare for ourselves, but we may not realize it as such. We may not be steeped in anger, frozen in fear, or depressed—in fact, we may even feel amused, contented, or happy at times—but inevitably we experience moments when we are aware of how limiting and oppressive our situation is. As if caught in a fog, we feel utterly powerless: It seems that we can't run fast enough, that if we call for help our tongues won't work or no one will listen, or that people who come to our aid are doing so for their own agendas, trampling over our boundaries and barging into our intimate space. Giving in to apathy, we block ourselves from imagining what our lives could be. Instead, we dwell on how we don't have enough time or money or how we're too fat or skinny to change anything, or we start to fantasize about someone or something rescuing us from our sadness and powerlessness.

At the moment of lucidity in a bad dream, when you recognize that you're in a terrifying situation, you abruptly find yourself with your eyes open, waiting for the fear and powerlessness to dissipate as you reassure yourself that you're safe now that you're back in "reality." But what happens if your nightmare is unfolding in your waking life? That moment of lucidity doesn't come to lift you out of the scene of your partner saying, "I don't love you anymore," or the doctor telling you, "I'm sorry, it's cancer." Your suffering feels completely real, and you don't see any way to transport yourself into a better reality.

Just like when you're asleep, the moment you're conscious of your waking nightmare is the moment you have the possibility of changing it. However, it's important to recognize that willpower and unflagging belief aren't enough to alter the facts of your material circumstances in any significant way. If it were that easy, you could simply build up your determination and intention to will yourself a winning lottery ticket and a perfect bill of health.

Fairy-tale fantasies also don't work because they involve dreaming from a place of being wounded or unhealed; in the end, the prince never shows up, or he turns back into a frog after the third kiss. But when you dream a new reality for yourself on the inside, events outside of you will begin to align with the change you've made internally. It might happen slowly, but you could also be surprised by how rapidly your circumstances shift. Moreover, by dreaming courageously—that is, living a life that's in sync with your soul's desire for peace, meaning, and happiness—you'll find yourself starting to feel joyous and fulfilled no matter what is going on around you. You'll stop feeling trapped in that nightmare.

Our Personal Nightmares

All of us are born with two piles of suitcases that we drag around with us: our psychological and genetic baggage. Both of these legacies are responsible for the scripts of our personal nightmares. Psychological issues get woven into the stories we tell about our lives and examine on the therapist's couch: Mother was too demanding, our self-esteem suffered, we never had faith in ourselves, and we're unable to be honest in our relationships or to persevere in our goals. These tales also impact our luminous energy field (LEF), the light body that encases our physical body as if it were a second skin. In fact, shamans see these as karmic issues, which they perceive energetically, as dark imprints in the LEF.

Your LEF organizes your body in the same way that the energy fields of a magnet organize iron filings on a piece of glass. However, your LEF also informs your thoughts, feelings, and behaviors; these, in turn, choreograph whom you're going to be attracted to, date, and marry. Ultimately, it's the information encoded in your LEF that predisposes you to a particular kind of job and boss and determines the themes that will surface in your relationship with your partner.

The LEF is the instrument through which you dream the world into being. It consists of light and vibration, so whatever you vibrate in your LEF, you create in the world. Your inability to forgive your mother and move on causes a mark in your LEF that remains there after the physical body dies, so it's carried into the next lifetime. This wound will draw you to the parents you'll be born through, in order to manifest the family that will allow you the opportunity to heal yourself of your karma. If you don't take advantage of the opportunity and choose instead to stay stuck in the same old belief of *Mom ruined my life,* or *The stork dropped me off at the wrong home,* the wound remains unhealed, you wind up with the reasons why you can't have what you want, and your nightmare continues (psychologists call this "the repetition compulsion"). You can decide to take advantage of the opportunity to heal, or you can remain trapped in the same old nightmare.

Shamans heal karmic wounds using specialized techniques for working with energy to clear the dark imprints in the LEF because those contain information that will produce disease. I've come to understand that DNA is the hardware that creates the body by manufacturing proteins, while the LEF is the software that provides the instructions to the system. When we clear the LEF, we're no longer doomed to relive the ailments of our parents or carry the old karmic baggage through lifetime after lifetime. We stop dragging the chains of our stories behind us. (A shaman might clear the imprint of a karmic wound from the LEF through "the Illumination Process," which I describe in detail in my earlier book *Shaman, Healer, Sage.*)

A wound in our energy body can show up in our physical body as well, at the level of organs and systems. It will even inform our DNA, creating a genetic legacy for our children. We all carry genes that predispose us to a variety of ailments, which will appear in our physical body if we live a lifestyle that's in alignment with our karmic wound. For example, if we carry the code for type 2 diabetes, it will manifest if we continue our family's tradition of rewarding and comforting ourselves with sugary and fatty foods.

I know a man who, like his father, drank too much, smoked heavily, and repressed resentment that his great career opportunity had slipped away from him. At age 59, the father had suffered a massive heart attack that killed him. At age 59, the son was diagnosed as having coronary heart disease but avoided the heart attack by undergoing quadruple bypass. The heart-disease gene had been passed along from father to son, but so had the psychological, karmic legacy: the behaviors of drinking, smoking, and emotional repression that were part of the nightmare belief of *I missed my chance.*

Not all illnesses are the work of karma—some are certainly caused by environmental toxins that affect us, while others are the result of destructive lifestyle choices and don't have a hereditary element. But whatever our genetic legacy is, we can prevent it from creating illness or other personal nightmares for us. We do so by healing the LEF through the practices of living in truth, cleaning up our river, and being ready to die at any instant, setting the scene for a new and better dream. (I will explain these practices in Part II.)

Our Cultural Nightmare

In addition to our individual nightmares, we share in the collective one of materialism and conformity. The American dream was once one of opportunity and freedom that was expressed in myriad ways. The inventors of blues, jazz, and rock and roll didn't have "freedom from financial worry," the freedom to choose from several colors of iPods, or any of the other so-called freedoms that advertisers promise us, but they did have the freedom to create daring and original music. Unfortunately, what was once a noble aim of achievement through hard work and determination has deteriorated into a cultural nightmare that produces mediocrity.

From babyhood forward, we're spoon-fed a set of expectations that most of us don't bother to question until the day we wake up and realize that our lives aren't working for us. Even with all the social changes we've gone through as a civilization in the last 50 years, we find ourselves easily buying into scripted ideas about how we should live our lives and measure our worth and happiness.

When we subscribe to the collective nightmare, we convince ourselves that we can avoid suffering by working hard to acquire a slightly better job, a slightly better home and car, a slightly better collection of stuff than the next guy has, and a slightly better-looking romantic partner than we feel we deserve. That is, we determine our happiness by how much progress we're making toward the big goal of lasting material fulfillment. If we can move from a rental apartment to a starter home to a big house on a huge lot before we're 35, it's a sign that we're living our lives well. We can feel good about ourselves for having achieved what is, after all, the *new* American dream.

We don't allow ourselves to think about whether the one particular lifestyle we've talked ourselves into is making us happy, or whether something radically different might be more fulfilling for us. If our forward momentum is lost—the spouse leaves, the job becomes hellish, a health crisis takes the attention and money that we'd earmarked for achieving our goal of happiness and wealth—we feel like failures. We measure ourselves by our achievements and productivity (by how much we're *doing*) instead of focusing on our emotional and spiritual growth and enjoying the process of learning, discovering, and maturing.

We've been taught that thinking about our problems and examining them from every angle will help us change our habits and create more fulfilling lives, but we can get just as stuck in the nightmare by *thinking* too much as we do by *doing* too much. One hundred years after Sigmund Freud introduced the world to psychoanalysis, we've built a common vocabulary to help us understand and talk about every one of our concerns, big or small. While it's great that we're more self-aware than we used to be, the so-called talking cure hasn't actually cured us of our fear . . . nor has it shown us how to live a life of courage.

The problem is that we're focused on problems! All of our energy goes into thinking about, worrying about, and trying to fix our concerns. What we should be doing is shifting our perception to a higher level so that we can tap into our courage and imagine a world that isn't beleaguered with issues—and actually dream it into being. When we operate from a higher level of consciousness, we stop perceiving *problems* and instead perceive *situations* that are neither good nor bad; they simply are. When we do so, we start to see that an opportunity lies in every situation if we simply look at it from a different level of awareness.

Remaining stuck in our minds (what I call the level of "jaguar") keeps us focused on trying to overcome our obstacles by creating security for ourselves in the material world. We think that financial success will protect us from harm: from being without food and shelter and from having to depend on others for our everyday needs. Unfortunately, these dreams are unsustainable—even if we built up a nest egg so big that it couldn't be spent in a lifetime, it wouldn't protect us from becoming terminally ill or losing a loved one in an accident. In addition, if everyone were to achieve the level of material wealth we think we should aspire to, the impact on the global environment would be devastating. Imagine everyone in India and China living with the largest that those of us in the United States do. The American dream of material excess isn't realistic in the long run, and it's not making Americans happy, anyway.

We also look to social success as a form of security, so we long to be loved and admired. In fact, many people today dream of being famous because they mistakenly believe that that's the ticket to lasting love and admiration. However, the cost of others' approval can be intolerably high. There is no security in the material world, no matter how much we'd like to believe that the opposite is true.

With courage of the soul, we don't define ourselves by big houses, nice cars, worldwide fame, or social position, yet we can still enjoy all of these. We consider the lilies of the field and how they neither toil nor spin, yet they thrive in beauty and abundance. Yes, we address our needs and attain some comfort in the material world, but mostly we're concerned with our soul's longing to make the most of our gifts and talents and participate in creating a better world. We dream the world we'd like to live in. Our dreams stop being goals we strive for and start becoming a way of life. They cease being rooted in fears of lack and scarcity and are instead rooted in love and abundance. And while the dreams of the soul serve our own needs as individuals, they also serve those of the world. These are sacred dreams—fresh, creative, and able to infuse us with passion and the courage to act.

Uncreative Dreams

Unlike sacred dreams, the goals we set for ourselves don't tend to be very creative. Hard as we try to figure out how to manifest happiness in our lives, we don't often have the courage or creativity to conceive of a radically different way of living. Rather than question the expectations we've been carrying with us since childhood, most of us simply go along with the nightmare of "mediacracy"; that is, a culture of conformity shaped by the media, which pretends to celebrate difference, diversity, and creativity but actually promotes belonging and security to an extreme. We become afraid to break out of the mold and do anything truly different.

That's not to say we don't want to think of ourselves as a cut above the rest. Author and radio personality Garrison Keillor poked fun at this fantasy about ourselves in his description of the utopian Lake Wobegon, a fictional small town in Minnesota where "all the children are above average." Of course it's impossible for everyone to be above average. We can't change the laws of statistics and bell curves: The bulge is in the middle, where most of us reside, not at the high end of intelligence or achievement. We could try to move the entire bell curve to the right so that everyone is a little more intelligent, creative, or productive (or has a little more of whatever quality we admire), but that wouldn't satisfy our need to feel "special."

We want to believe that "me and mine" are just lucky enough to be on the right side of that curve, in the above-average category for everything. This is the mentality that has led to the dumbing down of scholastic aptitude tests several times over the last few decades. Our college-bound teenagers seem to be doing better than ever before because their test scores are quite impressive. While professors aren't fooled one bit, we as a culture enjoy the false assurance that our kids are getting smarter.

Whenever doubt about our specialness—our above-average place on that bell curve—arises, we become vulnerable to the pervasive message of advertising: that we can regain our status by using our spending power. If we feel that we're becoming indistinguishable from the fellow next door, we're told that an easy solution can be found in obtaining a mass-marketed object that will capture our uniqueness and "personal style." We pull out our credit cards and start acquiring false symbols of our creativity, importance, and specialness.

I'm always fascinated by commercials for cars, which are essentially big machines that guzzle fossil fuels as we drive them from point A to point B. In the ads, they're magical vehicles that transport us to another world where attractive people fall all over us, trees sway in the breeze as we pass them by (even though in reality, vehicle exhaust is killing them), and the rock-and-roll songs of our youth pound through our ears, pumping us up with vitality. As one ad once promised, "This is not your father's Oldsmobile." We can make a statement about our personal sense of style with whatever this year's most daring and different automobile is.

Yet if we had any true originality, we wouldn't be driving at all. In Holland, 40 percent of the population rides bicycles to work, but Americans tend to think that bikes are for kids or recreation. We like our vehicles big, and we thoroughly embrace our car culture despite its cost. Imagining another way to get around seems impossible.

Similarly, we've convinced ourselves that we can't create meaning or joy without the hard work and competition that is represented by all the things in our display cases, shelves, closets, attics, basements, and garages. In the U.S., consumerism has become the new opium of the people—or perhaps the "new and improved" opium. To get us past our cynicism, advertisers and the media have cleverly repackaged consumerism. We don't just buy stuff, we buy *limited-edition* stuff. Yet if there are limited-edition dolls on the shelves of dollar stores, how rare and collectible could our treasured possessions possibly be?

And we don't just buy items to give ourselves status or to try to keep up with the Joneses. No, now we buy that which shows our impeccable taste and ability to stay on the cutting edge; we pride ourselves on knowing what the hottest new Website or gadget is. We don't fall for the old television commercials and print ads. We like our ads smaller, tailored to our specific demographic, and appearing on our personally designed home page. We enjoy advertising and being in the know about what we can buy. Recently, a Nielsen Company study of TV recorders such as TiVo found that contrary to advertisers' fears, people are watching almost half of commercials during playback rather than fast-forwarding past them.

We like to believe that this is not our father's consumerism, but it is . . . and it's just as hollow and unfulfilling now as it was then.

≈ ≈ ≈

When we become paralyzed in a nightmare, we don't have any notion about how we can enjoy a sense of purpose without meeting with everyone's approval. Mothers feel they have to be perfect, fathers feel they have to be everything their own fathers weren't, and young people feel they have to be on track in every area of their lives by the time their tenth high school reunion rolls around. We think that with the right reputation, we'll always have the security of being surrounded by people who care about us and shower us with admiration.

Looking outside ourselves to feel validated doesn't work very well. Even our staunchest admirers and supporters may not always be there, may be secretly jealous of us and quietly engaging in sabotage or betrayal, or may turn against us when we finally find the courage to live a more creative life. The more healthy and balanced we become, the more we'll attract people who mirror our health and balance, and the more our false friends will start to go away. But as long as we go along with the nightmare, our so-called supporters will expect us to stick to the status quo and avoid dreaming of a different life.

It's time to wake up from the nightmare we've been participating in, let go of the need to succeed in the mediocre mold, and create a more creative dream.

Self-fulfilling Prophecies

We perpetuate our personal and cultural nightmares when we don't recognize our role in co-creating reality. Our subconscious beliefs, which are often rooted in fear instead of courage, create self-fulfilling prophecies. Yet we don't understand the power of our expectations for good or bad.

In the 1960s, two social researchers named Robert Rosenthal and Lenore Jacobson did an experiment in a public elementary school in San Francisco. The administration agreed to allow the children to take a particular intelligence test; afterward, the researchers informed the teachers that the test had not only measured intelligence but also predicted which students could make great gains in intellectual ability.

In reality, the test did no such thing. The researchers had randomly chosen a few students' names and declared to the teachers that these were the boys and girls who would benefit enormously from their giftedness. A year later all the children took a second IQ test, and those who supposedly had tremendous potential for achievement did far better than their peers did. In fact, the teachers claimed that these students were better readers, better behaved, more engaged by school, more intellectually curious, and even more sociable than the others. The teachers had made their unconscious assumptions about these particular boys and girls a reality, and their expectations became a self-fulfilling prophecy.

Like these students, most of us get locked into a particular fate by the expectations our parents and culture have of us, whether they're positive or negative. After a short time, we internalize these beliefs and become a version of what we're expected to be—no matter if it's true to who we really are and what we really want. Some of us will rebel against society, but even so, we remain caught in the loop because rather than being creative, we're simply doing

31

the opposite of what we've been told to do. Continually engaging in knee-jerk rebellions is just another type of nightmare.

Much as we may chafe at conforming to the expectations of our culture, our parents, our social class, and our neighbors, we think it will be difficult to find the courage to truly defy them. After a while, usually when we're in our 20s, most of us give up and convince ourselves that everyone must be right—we don't have what it takes to accomplish our secret goals after all, and it's time to let go of our "childish fantasies." We buckle down and get serious about finding the right spouse and establishing all the symbols of the new American dream. Soon we start to feel depressed and trapped, but we keep living the same way and hoping that things will change. I once heard that the definition of *insanity* is "doing the same thing over again and expecting a different result." If so, we're all insane.

To envision with our eyes *and* hearts open, to co-create a new reality by courageously dreaming, we have to shed the expectations of our cultural nightmare. Otherwise, we'll manifest the same old wounds again and again, drawing to us situations and people who challenge us to heal our karma at last. Once we begin to wake up from the nightmare, we can weave creative dreams that aren't distorted by the failures we experienced in the past, and we'll no longer feel that we have to rearrange the people and situations in our lives in the hopes of fixing ourselves. Only when we realize that there's nothing in our lives that requires "fixing" will we be free to change.

Co-creating a New Reality

The secret to dreaming is that we can't solely focus on a new job or a new car or a new partner. When we try to do so, the dream backfires, and we wake up to that realization five years or two children later. We cannot dream just the small picture—rather, we have to come up with an entirely new world, and then all the details will take care of themselves. None of us can micromanage creation; we can only set great forces into motion. Whenever the details of our vision aren't working out, it's a sign that we're not dreaming big enough.

When you dream a new world, your co-creator is the universe, the creative force that causes trees to grow from seedlings and galaxies to grow from stardust. It's the force that took you from sperm and unfertilized egg to human baby and designed your DNA, as well as the mysterious trigger that tells each cell what its job is, whether it's supposed to specialize in transporting oxygen as a red blood cell or produce hormones as a gland cell. You tap into the intelligence of the universe, and it conspires on your behalf to organize the natural world to mirror back your dream.

There is no question that we humans have created the chaos and beauty of the world we live in: It's our dream manifested. From manicured parks to overpopulation to industrial pollution, from crowded streets in China to the melting ice caps to the polar bear in the Central Park Zoo, everything we perceive is the creation of humanity working in conjunction with (and often at odds with) the universe. We've been true to our mandate in the Bible to take of the plants and animals as we see fit, and the natural world has responded to our choices. Our footprint is everywhere.

We've fashioned the modern world with all of its beauty and terror. We've also shaped and molded the natural world with its whales and butterflies to fit our needs, but we didn't actually create it. Or did we? Some physicists have postulated "the anthropic principle" to explain the strange and extremely unlikely coincidences that had to occur for there to be intelligent life. It's as if the universe had conspired to create this perfect and highly improbable balance of forces that would lead to life.

Creationists explain this unlikelihood by saying that a god choreographed the whole dance of existence, while evolutionists say that we should assume the sun, the earth, and the life that evolved on our planet are all the result of random events. As humans we tend to perceive things dualistically, as if one camp is right and the other is wrong, but dualism is simply the result of our desire to force reality into a neat little package. Perhaps both sides only see part of the story—maybe what happened is that back when all was a void, as part of the force of creation, our consciousness participated in the glorious work of art known as the universe. Consciousness expressed itself in the physical world as the Milky Way, the asteroid belts, and the perfect mix of elements that lead to the creation of human beings with the ability to ponder how we got here. It could be that we're part of the Creator *and* the creation simultaneously, and we participate in a dance of evolution that's brilliantly logical and whimsical at the same time.

While the question of if we invented ourselves is an interesting one, most of us are concerned more with whether we can dream the world differently at a personal level. Can we craft the families, lifestyles, meaning, and purpose we wish for; or are we at the mercy of forces much larger than ourselves that sculpt and shape our fate? Are we another cog in the wheel of a machine, or do we belong to ourselves and have a personal destiny we can fashion and hone?

It may seem that all the evidence is stacked against individuals having any say about the course of our own destiny, that we're falling for an illusion that provides us a false sense of being in the captain's seat when we're really on a rudderless ship. We can gracefully accept what fate bestows on us, or we can shift our perception. Could we have dreamed the universe into being yet not be able to make an iota of difference in our own lives?

We can steer the ship of our life and even summon the wind and change its direction, but to do so requires quiet acts of courage. It requires letting go of the need to move the winds for our own purposes and instead choose to move them for the greater good of all. It requires that we accept responsibility for what we change instead of ducking the consequences. And most of all, it requires that we be careful what we wish for, because what we dream, we will create.

Reality and Perception

We go about our lives trusting that there are things that everyone can agree upon. A piece of wood is a piece of wood, and humans all over the world understand this. We also recognize its properties: It has weight yet can float, it can be burned when it's dry, and so on. According to Newtonian physics, a branch of science that explains natural phenomena, we can predict how quickly the piece of wood will fall if dropped from a height. There's no great mystery in that log that we can see, touch, smell, taste, and even hear as it falls to the ground. We understand and agree upon the fact that wood is a solid object with certain characteristics. At the level of awareness that most of us operate in, wood is very real and very hard, and we don't want a big piece of it dropping on top of us.

In contrast, in quantum mechanics, the branch of science that explains how our world works at the subatomic level, the old ideas about reality fly out the window. That same piece of wood, for instance, does not have fixed characteristics. The tiniest unit of matter, smaller than an atom, is a particle; thus, the wood is mostly made up of air that is filled with a buzzing cloud of continually vibrating particles. A particle is a tricky little piece of "stuff"—if we observe its location at any given moment, we have no way of measuring its speed. If we measure the particle's velocity, it becomes impossible to determine where it is. Then, as I mentioned earlier, the very nature of the particle often changes when it's observed: It may take on the characteristics of a wave, the smallest unit of energy, and then turn back into a particle, the smallest unit of matter.

Given this very different "reality" at the subatomic level, is it correct to say that we human beings are solid creatures, made up of air and a bunch of buzzing particles; or are we energy beings, made up of a lot of waves of energy? Could we be both, continually flipping from one state to the other? Is a piece of wood a solid object, or is that just how we happen to perceive it? What would happen if we perceived it as a collection of waves, as a collection of energy?

I'm not suggesting that by changing our perception, a piece of wood will magically change its nature in the physical world (even though some of the shamans I've met claim that this is the case). If it falls on top of us, we'll feel pain—that's a fact at the physical level. But at a different level of reality, something else is going on when the piece of wood hits us. We get to explain the experience using thoughts, feelings, and metaphors. We determine the piece of wood's significance in our lives by writing a story.

We might think that it's a dead branch loosened from the tree by a strong wind, falling down on top of us. We might feel that it's a damned hard piece of wood causing us pain and making us upset. We might perceive that it's a wake-up call because it takes us out of our thoughts and back into the physical world where we need to be at the moment, so we get ourselves out of the windstorm and back into shelter before an even bigger branch hits us. The piece of wood may be a reminder of the fact that we're not paying attention in life. Any or all of these stories could be true: We have the power to determine which one we want to create to explain being conked on the head by a falling branch.

Most of the time the facts we're dealing with feel just as solid as a piece of wood. The facts might be that we have small children dependent on us and a salary that's not enough to cover our monthly bills. The facts might be that we experience low and high sugar levels in our blood and have a disease that doctors call "diabetes," and if we don't pay attention to our meals, exercise, and insulin levels, we may cause long-term damage to our body. These facts don't disappear in the material world any more than the piece of wood does. However, our facts are not our stories— they're just the building blocks, the words we piece together to write our tale of being a victim of poverty and poor health or of being a survivor who overcomes obstacles, manages difficulties, maintains an optimistic attitude, and gives our children an abundance of love. Our situation might be a difficult one, but it's only a nightmare if we choose to make that our reality. By taking the facts and writing a new story with them, we can script a different experience of reality.

~~~~~~

CHAPTER TWO

The Scripts of Our Nightmares

We don't see things as they are;
we see them as we are.
— ANAÏS NIN

Researchers have found that our minds naturally create narratives around the facts of our lives, and the way we tell our personal stories strongly influences how we see ourselves as well as how we behave. When the recurring theme of our tales is triumph over adversity, and we describe troubles as appearing unexpectedly and recall how we vanquished them, we're able to experience well-being and feel hopeful about the future. We move forward with confidence and take risks. However, when our stories focus on the dark lining in every cloud—the events that "ruined" each moment of happiness—we're likely to experience mood problems and feel unhappy, powerless, and apathetic. This chapter will help to shed some light on the negative scripts we've become slaves to.

Trapped in the Three Archetypes

None of us start out as pessimists. In fact, most of us once believed that we could enjoy a Disneyesque tale of wonder and joy, with endless fun all day and fireworks every night. But then life happened.

If we examine the stories we tell as adults, we almost always find that they're variations on ancient themes that have been represented throughout the ages in fables and fairy tales. As we grew up, we unknowingly became trapped in one of three archetypal stories, all of which promised us joy but ended up delivering misery.

The three fairy tales that become core scripts for our bad dreams are:

1. The story of King Midas, which turns into the nightmare titled "I Don't Have Enough."

2. The story of the Lion King, which turns into the nightmare titled "I'm Too Old and My Time Has Passed."

3. The story of Cinderella, which turns into the nightmare titled "I'm Too Wounded to Have Power."

Once we recognize that we're living according to one of these archetypal scripts, we can consciously choose to rip it up and start over with a new story. But first we have to be honest about just how much we're conforming to a fairy-tale fantasy about what will make us feel happy and fulfilled.

King Midas's Golden Touch

According to the myth, King Midas was a good ruler who exhibited hospitality toward Silenus (the teacher and faithful companion of Dionysus) when he got drunk and fell asleep in Midas's rose garden. Dionysus, who is best known as the god of wine and revelry, wanted to reward the king for his generosity toward his friend—but this god was also known as a guardian of the mystery traditions, representing the holy ecstasy of creativity and spirituality. When Dionysus asked Midas, already a wealthy ruler, what gift he desired, the king chose a material one rather than one of the arts or of the spirit, which Dionysus could have bestowed upon him. The god reluctantly gave the mortal the gift of the golden touch: Whatever the greedy king touched would turn to pure gold, making him the richest man in the world.

Midas was thrilled to watch the grass under his feet become gilded and see the creek he dipped his hand in transform into a flowing river of wealth. It was all wonderful until Midas got hungry and decided it was time for dinner. He immediately spat out the wine in his goblet, for it had turned to liquid gold, completely undrinkable. And when he touched the food on his plate, he instantly rendered it inedible. Midas's blessing quickly became a curse, as no one dared come close to him for fear that they'd be turned into a statue of gold, and no matter how much wealth he attained, he was doomed to be hungry, lonely, and dissatisfied.

In one version of the myth, after Midas has been miserable for many years and living in isolation from the world, his daughter pleas with him to pray to Dionysus to be relieved of this curse. The god tells him that he must bathe in a holy river and return his gift to the waters so that his wealth can now fertilize the earth. This indeed rids Midas of the golden touch, and as an old man he is finally able to enjoy the beauty of his kingdom.

The story of King Midas is a metaphor for the sense of lack we feel in our lives. Like that mortal man, we must accept that there's no escape from this harsh reality: Nothing and no one can fill the void inside that's created by the belief that we don't have enough—enough money, beauty, youth, charm, love, power, or what have you.

Like the king, we all incur the favor of Dionysus during our youth. The festive aspect of the god grants us our wishes in our early life, so we freely engage in revelry and lovemaking and living it up. But then we're faced with a need to grow up and mature because we can't continue partying all of our lives. Those who try to do so slowly enter a downward spiral of decay and degeneration as the party turns ugly. Most of us tend to choose the same wish that Midas made—the golden touch. We figure out how we can gain position, wealth, and influence; and the god seems to grant us our wishes as we begin to experience financial and career success.

But the golden touch we acquire comes at the cost of losing a part of our soul, the part represented by Dionysus in his role as the keeper of the mystery traditions. We begin to forget about the other type of wealth he could bestow on us: the ability to experience riches that are spiritual, not physical. We turn away from the "high" experienced by those who are actively involved in living artistically and creatively. We don't indulge in the ecstasy of meditation and prayer; instead, we gravitate toward the "intoxication" of wine and medications that dull our senses.

As in the myth, we have to recognize that we hunger and thirst for a different kind of sustenance. Otherwise, people will turn away from us just as they turned away from Midas in the story, and we'll find ourselves increasingly isolated and surrounded only by the things we've accumulated. Then at some point we may pray for help, recognizing that we need to use our riches and talents to replenish the earth. We may seek to experience the tremendous joy, energy, and excitement of creativity and spirituality—using these gifts to act in ways that affect the world for the better, planting seeds of change.

If we don't follow this course of action, however, we fall into the nightmare of believing that if we can just attain more material wealth, stature, or importance, we will finally be satisfied. When we don't seek help from the divine, who can guide us in removing our curse, our touch begins to turn everything into dirt. (If you look back at your own life, you'll see when you had the golden touch and then lost it and tried desperately to regain it.)

We all experience that golden touch at times and long to regain our youth, our popularity, our reputation—or whatever it was that we were convinced was the key to happiness. Yet unlike King Midas, once we realize we've lost that touch, there's no one to rescue us from our angst. We get stuck waiting for someone to save us from our curse. When the marriage fails or the company we invested in goes bust, we experience desperation, panic, and resentment. We take another spin around the mall or online dating site in the vain hope that we can acquire something or someone to ease our misery.

When we fear that we don't have enough—enough time, money, friends, love, power, and so on—we are participating in the nightmare of scarcity. Many of us go shopping every day, not because we have to but because we want to believe that if we buy something, we'll have "enough." We'll buy too many clothes, toys, and gifts for our children and friends because we hope that our generosity will be "enough" to win their approval and gratitude. We'll redecorate or stretch ourselves to cover a too-costly mortgage on a colossal house, all the while wishing that our home would be "good enough" for us to entertain in and impress the neighbors with. But no matter how much we spend or how well we can sniff out bargains, we can never have enough.

The error is thinking that we can fix our "problem" of not being or having enough with the remedy of material abundance. Accumulating lots of stuff and then spending more money out of a feeling of lack won't cure the Midas curse. Instead, just like the king himself, we can choose to dream a life in which we're enough to be happy and satisfied, regardless of what we have or own.

To awaken from a nightmare like this, you have to reject the poorly written script that dictates, "If I had _____, I could create lasting happiness." Only then can you imagine what a healthy, vibrant, fulfilling life would be like. The longer and more intently you hold on to the vision that you are enough and are surrounded by plenty, the easier it is to begin to manifest your dream in the physical world.

The Lion King's Moment of Reclamation

Another myth we unwittingly re-create in our lives is that of the Lion King. The story, which was turned into a Disney movie and a stunning musical, follows a lion cub who escapes his evil uncle's plot to kill him and take possession of his father's throne. The youngster flees into the bush, where he grows up in the company of a lowly warthog and other creatures of the forest. Eventually, he forgets that he's the heir to a kingdom, until his beloved finds him and reminds him of his ancestry and possible greatness. The young lion then returns to challenge his uncle and reclaim his royal birthright and power.

This nightmare, also known as "My Time Will Come," is one that many men in our culture fall prey to as they long for the moment when their importance will be recognized. Or the nightmare has them believing that *the next deal I'm working on is the big one that will bring me to my rightful place in life.*

A man will frequently look to his partner for the inspiration and motivation to manifest his greatness, buying into the adage that behind every successful man is a wonderful woman. A man may look for a woman who will give him confidence or inspire him to be kingly. Yet this tends to be a daunting task for a woman, for she has to mother her partner while retaining her attraction to him and raising him from a cub to a prince to a king. The woman who signs up for this kind of task must put her own life on hold and live vicariously through her man's success. And if the male lion doesn't succeed, he blames the female for the failure.

Men are not the only ones who become trapped in this nightmare—women can be seduced by the call to prominence as well. As everyone has both a feminine and a masculine aspect to his or her psyche, the masculine side is particularly vulnerable to the nightmare of the Lion King. So when a woman succumbs to the power of this myth, she has to enlist the feminine side of her psyche to come to her aid, as she has no external "wife" to support her in her quest for attainment. This will come at a high price: The nurturing feminine side will be compromised and will harden, causing her to eventually become bitter at being exclusively in service to the masculine side that seeks achievement and recognition.

There is another way that a woman succumbs to this myth. She might see the potential for greatness in the man she loves, while he's unable or unwilling to recognize it himself. Try as she may to help her partner grow and succeed, he continues to refuse her help. This is a blow that's very difficult for a woman to recover from, because after a while she'll develop contempt for her partner and lose all respect for him.

The Lion King nightmare is a deadly trap for men or women who feel as if life owes them something or has some secret worldly eminence in store for them. Of course life does offer us the possibility of greatness, but it's of the creative and spiritual variety. When we don't rise to our inner sense of potential, we're left with the feeling expressed by Marlon Brando in *On the Waterfront* . . . that he could have been a "contender."

Not recognizing the nightmare, a man caught up in the Lion King fantasy will focus on his nemesis, represented in the myth by the evil uncle. He'll convince himself that if he could only eliminate the horrible and dominant male who has the position and the power he wants, he could reclaim his rightful throne, so he bides his time and awaits his opportunity . . . but it never comes. This man could be his father, boss, or even a romantic rival.

Eventually, we realize that unlike the young Lion King, we're caught in a nightmare entitled "I'm Too Old and My Time Has Passed." The reason is because the fairy tale never comes true in real life. We won't regain the kingdom because we can never be 22 again, with a world of possibilities stretching out before us. Biding our time, we're overcome by the fear that all the doors are closing. We find ourselves fretting about how we're old and tired and can no longer compete. There's always someone younger than we are who will take a lower salary or can offer a more buffed body to a potential romantic partner.

Many of my clients are baby boomers in their mid-50s who desperately want to reinvent their lives yet stubbornly hang on to the nightmare of "I'm Too Old and My Time Has Passed." They're afraid to let go of it and live creatively or take risks. When they do break out of this fairy tale, they find that their most creative days are still ahead of them.

Then there's what a psychologist friend of mine who specializes in commitment issues told me: that as pessimistic as her clients in their 30s, 40s, and 50s are about finding companionship, those expressing the greatest amount of anxiety about the subject are the ones in their 20s. The belief that time has ticked away and it's too late to achieve one's dream can hit us at any age and stop us cold with fear and self-doubt. My mother found love at age 79, but I bet that when she was 22 she felt threatened by all those nubile 17-year-olds she believed she was competing against.

We feel old not because we're a particular age, but because we believe that time has passed us by in some way. We don't understand computers or video games, nor can we relate to the movies of this generation. We stop discovering new things or challenging ourselves to take risks. Instead, we turn on the oldies station and declare that all the music today is dreadful. We start forwarding snarky e-mails about our failing memories and stiff joints to friends, for we're convinced that the inevitable decline has already started.

Yet not everyone buys into the idea that the older you get, the more you age. I know 80-year-olds who are a lot more fun to be around than many 30-year-olds because they're embracing life with passion. They feel that their best years are still ahead of them, that the best books have yet to be written and the best music has yet to be composed. That they have stiffer knees or less physical stamina may be facts, but they're not part of a story called "I'm Slowly Passing Away into the Shadows of Death, and It's All Downhill from Here."

There are second chances in life (and even third, fourth, and fifth chances), but when we're caught in the Lion King nightmare, we feel that's not true. Remember that the nightmare is what happens when the fairy tale doesn't end the way it was supposed to. Therefore, as much as we might want to seize on a new opportunity, when it comes along we can't find the courage to act because we're stuck in the old refrain of "Oh, I'm no good at that. I tried it once before and failed." The fear of failing utterly paralyzes us. The question we should be asking ourselves isn't "Is it too late to begin living a life of passion and purpose?" but "How do I start today?"

It's true that not all opportunities will come back around. For example, you really can't become a star ballerina at the age of 42 if you've never taken a ballet lesson before, but if you're willing to get to the core of your dream—such as the aspiration to dance and perform—you'll start to see ways in which you can manifest it. You don't have to create a nightmare in which your life is over long before your body begins to deteriorate. You can retain a thirst for new experiences and a sense of wonder at life itself.

Cinderella's Glass Slipper

In the Cinderella story, a good-hearted and hardworking girl is so mistreated by her stepmother and stepsisters that they make her life hell. But one magical night, Cinderella's fairy godmother rescues her from her misery by changing a pumpkin into a carriage, mice into coachmen, and Cinderella's rags into a gorgeous gown and glass slippers. The girl then has the opportunity to attend the palace ball, win the love of the prince, and become queen of the land.

Although Cinderella has been hurt by her family, the prince doesn't see her as a wounded girl; he sees her as a beautiful and worthy dancing partner. Thus, when the moment comes that the magic wears off and Cinderella flees into the night with only the clothes on her back, the prince lovingly cradles the glass slipper she leaves behind and vows to find his princess no matter what it takes. He searches high and low, ultimately placing the slipper on the slender foot of a poor girl in rags—and when he discovers that she is the beautiful woman he fell for that moonlit night, he happily whisks her away to the life of wealth and comfort she deserves.

Many a woman thinks of herself as a modern-day Cinderella, abused and overlooked but fated to experience her moment of magic and be rescued by a handsome and wealthy prince (or at least a glamorous job). Unfortunately, when the magic wears off at midnight and the prince turns out to be a frog with a drinking problem and a checkered past, there is no rescue. No one comes because the girl is too hurt to find that glass slipper, claim it as hers, and demand the keys to the castle. Cinderella gets stuck in the nightmare known as "I'm Too Wounded to Have Any Power over My Life."

As in the fairy tale, a woman trapped in this archetype will often blame other females for her woes: The evil stepmother who forced her to be someone other than her real self becomes the mom who never really appreciated her wonderful daughter. The cruel stepsisters are now other women who squash Cinderella's potential by telling her that she's not good enough to win the heart of a prince or achieve a life of power in a palace. Women who are suffering because of their own wounds will often act catty or competitive, going so far as to be downright vicious as they try to make themselves feel better by telling their friend that she's dreaming too big. Even women who want to be loving and supportive to other women may reinforce their female friends' destructive and disempowering beliefs, which warn that "there are no good men" and "it's a man's world, so be prepared to suffer."

A male variation on the Cinderella theme is that of Spider-Man, Superman, and other comic-book superheroes who are lucky enough to acquire magical powers and the admiration of all the citizens of Earth. Yet they can't have loving romantic partnerships because any women who fall for them are doomed to be destroyed. Lois Lane and all those other girls have to be pushed away lest they get hurt—and the superheroes can't ever let them know how much they pine for these women.

This story, which gets recycled in the comics and the movies, resonates for the man who can't imagine that there might be a woman who can accept a superhero with problems and manage quite nicely. Instead, the belief of *Despite the appearance that I'm powerful, I'm too wounded to find happiness—I'll just screw things up and make myself miserable again* locks him into yet another nightmare of victimhood.

Breaking Away from the Nightmare of Victimhood and Powerlessness

Being hurt emotionally is a fact for many people, as pain is a part of human existence. However, becoming a victim as a result of this wounding is a framing of that fact. We take our pain and create an exotic story of suffering and victimhood. It's not enough that our parents got divorced when we were seven and we didn't get to see Dad as often as we wanted to; rather, we tell ourselves, our potential romantic partners, and our therapists that "I have intimacy issues ever since my father left my mother, my siblings, and me all alone." We love to add details to flesh out the story and create a drama that traps us.

The story of victimhood has become ubiquitous, creating a culture of powerlessness that expresses itself in many ways. We talk about our issues and our problems with near strangers so that they'll understand why we just don't have it in us to perform difficult tasks such as waiting our turn or tending to our own needs instead of expecting someone else to attend to them. The self-help movement is rife with people who spend all their energy exploring themselves and their "issues," honing their stories again and again rather than breaking out of them. As a woman I met at a party told me by way of introducing herself, "I almost didn't come tonight because I suffer from low self-esteem."

Even those who ridicule the culture of victimhood like to define themselves as victims of other people who only claim to be victims. We compete to see who has the heavier load to carry: Who suffered more? Whose aches and pains trump? Who has a better excuse for not being the first to say "I'm sorry"? We rifle through the file in our mind labeled "Stories of My Wounds" and pull out a stack of them to wave them at others, claiming that our stories prove we deserve pity, special accommodations, and relief from responsibility in our relationships.

Validating our pain can help us discover our strengths and learn valuable lessons, but when we start colluding in the nightmare of being so wounded that we can't recover, we become emotionally, mentally, and spiritually crippled. Once again, we buy into our own powerlessness and become paralyzed.

Three Stock Characters

To be a victim requires a perpetrator. If we want to feel sorry for ourselves, we have to have a bully to blame for our woeful state of powerlessness, and if we can't identify one, we have to invent one. After we've found our bully, we have to invent the possibility of rescue. We need a *deus ex machina,* or "god from the machine," who can drop down into our lives and fix all of our problems. We long for a daddy, a Prince Charming, or an angel of compassion to rescue us.

The Earthkeepers say that all the stories we write to explain our reality feature the conquistador, the Indian, and the priest. The conquistador is a bad guy who persecutes the hapless Indian victim, whose only hope is to be rescued by the noble priest. These stock characters behave predictably and create the same tired plots; until we get rid of them, we'll find ourselves continually caught in those very plots.

In our own personal stories and fairy tales, we use the similar archetypes of bully, victim, and rescuer: In the story of King Midas, the bully is Dionysus; the victim is the king; and the rescuer is Midas's young daughter, who tells him to plead his case before Dionysus. In the Lion King, the bully is the evil uncle, the victim is the cub, and the rescuer is his beloved. In the story of Cinderella, the bullies are the stepmother and stepsisters, the victim is Cinderella, and the rescuer is the noble prince. Notice how all of these stories are written from the point of view of the victim. By the same token, we tend to script our nightmares with ourselves as victims of some cruel person or terrible event. The problem is that every time we paint ourselves this way, we're writing stories of powerlessness and apathy. The victim in us depicts the reasons why we cannot have what we want.

But sometimes the story is written from the point of view of the bully, particularly by men, who like to think of themselves as being powerful, righteous warriors who are justified in their harshness or vindictiveness. When we find ourselves boasting about the great deal we just closed, how we vanquished our adversary, or how we conquered an illness, we're identifying with the conquistador. Then again, we may choose to write the story from the point of view of the rescuer, because we want to congratulate ourselves on how we're saving our partners from themselves or nobly sacrificing our lives and our independence for our children.

In reality, all three characters are interchangeable and we shift between roles, going from victim to noble rescuer of other victims, or from noble rescuer to angry and self-righteous bully. For example, after the 9/11 terrorist attacks on the twin towers in New York City and the Pentagon in Washington, D.C., the entire planet was behind the United States. We Americans had tremendous political goodwill around the globe and, along with most everyone else, thought of ourselves as the victims of a tragic event.

Yet in just a few short months we squandered that goodwill—and today people in several parts of the world perceive the U.S. as a bully that's throwing its weight around and hurting innocent citizens while single-handedly trying to rid the earth of the "bad guys" and make it a safe place for democracy. Meanwhile, many Americans justify torture and violating civil rights because they see themselves as righteous warriors against terrorism. None of these stories—of Americans as victims, rescuers, or bullies—seems to be helping the planet conjure up a better dream than an endless cycle of suffering and revenge.

As you do the following exercise, you'll start to discover how you cast yourself in the three archetypal roles and begin to recognize how pointless and paralyzing the tired old stories featuring your own King Midas, Cinderella, and Lion King are.

Exercise: Discovering the Bully, Victim, and Rescuer in Your Story

Write the story of the latest outrage you've suffered, sparing no detail as you tell your tale of woe. Embellish it with your plan for revenge, describing just what you'll do to turn the tables and transform your perpetrator into the victim. Explain how you're going to rescue yourself or someone else from this or a similar situation.

Your story might read something like this:

> *My son's idiot soccer coach refused to let him play his favorite position. Yesterday my son was crying about it. I was furious and told him that the next time he has practice, I'll tell that coach just what I think of his stupid decision to let another kid play that position.*

Or . . .

> *My ex-husband lost the important papers we need to file our taxes this year, and my accountant is telling me that we have to reconstruct them or may get audited. I called up my ex and told him that I was tired of his irresponsibility screwing up my life, and he called me a bitch and hung up on me. I am terrified of being audited and am ready to kill him. No matter what I do, he's got the power to ruin my life and make me miserable.*

Now write out your list of characters, identifying who's portraying the roles of victim, bully, and rescuer. Notice that the same person may play different roles in different parts of the story, as the victim becomes so angry that he turns into a bully, or the unappreciated rescuer becomes the victim. Look closely at your story and ask yourself if anyone in it is taking on a role that isn't a victim, bully, or rescuer.

What is the title of your tale? It should be the name of your problem, so the first story might be "They Are Not Being Fair to My Child," while the second could be "My Ex Is Making Me Miserable." The title is your way of defining the facts of your account in such a way as to create a problem.

The real problem is that you're confusing your story for reality. Your narrative is a nightmare of suffering that you can't escape as long as you hang on to it. Your ex is not making you miserable; *you* are making yourself miserable. He is just being himself, which is why you divorced him in the first place. But even though you're no longer living with him, he's still playing the role you cast him in.

Look closely at your story and think about whether there's a way to solve your problem within that story through some action you might take. Would this action cause you to once again play the role of victim, bully, or rescuer? If so, you're simply writing yet another chapter in your nightmare that you'll have to live out.

In a later exercise, you'll write a new script for this story—one in which you don't take on the role of victim, bully, or rescuer; and no one else does either.

Ridding Yourself of Karmic Chains

The stories you subscribe to become your waking nightmares, and they blind you to your power to dream and create. They become your karmic baggage. Like a ghost dragging heavy chains behind him, you carry the weight of your sagas everywhere you go; they manifest again and again in your life, although the details may vary here and there. In fact, clinical psychologists will secretly admit that they sometimes struggle to stay awake during their sessions with patients because while their clients believe their personal stories are endlessly dramatic, they're actually the same shopworn tales that keep being retold.

Our narratives form the basis of our personal mythology. The father trying to rescue his son from the soccer coach is most likely using his child to try to soothe his own story of not being treated fairly in his youth. The woman whose ex-husband is making her miserable and is fantasizing about revenge is trying to appease the feeling of being out of control in her own life through her former spouse. Both are using the "other" to try to heal their own wounds.

While we sometimes have the courage to break free of our psychological and karmic stories, usually we simply end the situation and re-create it in another area of our lives. The new boss is as much of a bully as the old boss was—he just persecutes us in a slightly different way. The new girlfriend morphs into that wretched ex-wife of ours. Or we revisit our troubled relationship with Dad through the one we have with our son, our business partner, or even our President.

The way to break those karmic chains is to let go of the countless reasons you can't have what you want. Reasons, such as those that follow, are the heart of your story:

- Because my parents were critical, I can't feel good about myself. I am not "enough."

- Because I've been discriminated against, I missed out on the opportunities that would have allowed me to make my life better. I am old and my time has passed.

- Because I can't have what I want, I'm too wounded to create happiness for myself.

As you look at the seemingly unalterable facts of your life, you might say, "But I'm not making excuses. These facts are real." They may indeed be very real to you. However, it's easy to confuse the past with the present and the future, perceiving facts in a fixed reality when they may not be facts at all. Your "facts" are simply beliefs rooted in memories.

Your brain doesn't distinguish between what's happening in the present moment and what you're experiencing as you retell a story about the past. Neuroscientists are discovering that at a synaptic level, a real and a recalled event both register in the neocortex and the limbic system in the same way, with the same intensity. Career athletes know that to perform at their best, they need to start by visualizing themselves completing a perfect ski run or hitting the golf ball onto the green. Athletes who see themselves receiving a gold medal don't do as well as those who visualize themselves successfully running the course because the former are dreaming wishfully while the latter are laying the neural pathways for a successful run.

In fact, every time you relive an old hurt, it reinforces that synaptic pathway. Thus, whenever you retell the story called "My Third-Grade Teacher Told Me I Was Lazy and Wouldn't Amount to Anything," the anguish you feel isn't from the old wounds being reopened, it's from the new pain being created as you spin the yarn. You may think you're simply venting and getting rid of the old shame and anger, but your brain knows otherwise. You give the account life as you infuse it with energy and make it your reality today.

In other words, the more we repeat woeful tales to ourselves, the deeper we etch the grooves along those neural pathways. Eventually they become like canals into which our experiences and perceptions drain constantly, following the path of least resistance. We channel much of our sensory input and the way we read the world along these neural trails; thus, we superimpose the face of our ex-wife over our new girlfriend or that of our evil mother over our new boss.

Throughout the years, many artists, mythmakers, and religious leaders have instinctively understood that the brain cannot tell the difference between a "real" and a "perceived" event. They created public rituals or performances that allowed a community to bring to the surface hidden feelings of aggression, hurt, or reconciliation. The Kabuki theater of Japan is an excellent example: Kabuki originated in the early 1600s as a form of comedy, but after the terrible disgrace endured by the Japanese after World War II, Kabuki performers became rigid and constrained, with truncated movements and almost painful gestures on the part of the performers to represent the loss suffered by their nation. Similarly, Greek theater provided healing and relief for the people. Even the Catholic Mass at its core provides a release for the shadow elements—the pain, the suffering, and the violence that lies within all of us that we hide in the shadows of our awareness because it makes us very uncomfortable. If you look closely at the Catholic Mass, it's filled with imagery of great anguish being transformed into bliss by the Resurrection of Christ. Many religious rituals allow the brain to acknowledge, feel, and work through our painful emotions in an archetypal way.

When you're unable to let go of your suffering, it becomes like a demon you haven't exorcised, a crazed monster who's waiting to be unleashed. You can cast out that demon by naming it—perhaps something like "My Need to Make My Ex-wife Understand That She's an Irrational Freak"—and then ordering it to get out of your psyche. But it can't be banished until it's replaced by something new and more empowering. For example, if the phone rings and caller ID shows that it's your ex-wife on the line, you don't have to pull out the old script and start thinking, *Oh no, it's her. She's going to tell me how she thinks I neglect the kids, and I'm going to feel angry and hurt. That's what she always does.* Instead, you can set the scene for a new story to unfold, casting yourself in the role of a man who takes responsibility for himself but doesn't take on other people's burdens. You can open up to the possibility that your ex won't attack you because you're no longer wearing the bull's-eye on your behind.

Making the choice to break out of the old script, even in a small moment such as this, takes great courage. It requires that you observe the tale that arises instantaneously and let go of your need to feel safe and secure, since that need causes you to don your battle gear. You know very well that your former spouse may start accusing you of something, but by assuming that's the case, you set yourself up for that script to play out. Because you have a long-established dynamic with her, she'll pick up her cue to play out the script, in the same way that a musician will hear the opening bars to a piece of music and join in instinctively. You'll have her at *hello,* and neither of you will miss a line in your script.

When you have the courage to drop your negative expectations and say, "Hello, and how are you today?" and truly allow yourself to be open to whatever comes next, you wake up from the nightmare. You can listen to the sarcastic accusation she hurls at you, but you won't cast her as a bully and yourself as a victim. You won't even be tempted to take on the more noble and seemingly powerful role of rescuer, pointing out how she's caught in her drama and hoping to fix her. Instead, you can come up with a new, better dream called "My Ex-wife and I Are Creating Peace" and invite her to participate in it. She might turn you down, but that's her decision. You can choose differently.

The Fleeting Nature of Facts

Because we have such a strong need for familiarity, we resist admitting that people and situations can change. *All facts are impermanent*—when you accept this, you can let go of that frightening feeling that you're powerless to reinvent your life or change your circumstances. No matter how fixed reality seems at this moment, remember that even glaciers move over time. Facts are so dynamic that reality is continually in motion. When reality seems to be frozen in place, it's an illusion created by our stories. The co-worker who we say torments us moves on to another company, but we hold on to our resentment about that day two years ago when he spilled coffee on our project. We cling to our perceptions long after the actual facts have changed, and that petrifies reality for us.

One of my clients overcame a severe health crisis yet hung on to the belief that the purpose of her life was to survive, to make it through one more day without succumbing to her disease. She regained her health, but thinking about her future and what she wanted to do next with her life was extremely difficult for her. She had to let go of her old story (that she was ill and needed every ounce of courage and strength she had to fight her condition) and embrace the new set of facts (that she was healthy and had a future in the physical world). She'd become familiar with her role as a survivor and a fighter, but now she had to discover meaning without the need for illness.

The older we get, the more we see that change happens, sometimes mysteriously and with the strangest timing. We'll feel completely stuck in a job, analyze the situation endlessly, and finally come to the conclusion that we have no options whatsoever. We insist that the only way to remain in our career is to put up with the abusive boss at work because the only other companies with similar positions are located in a different city, and our child won't agree to move. Then to our surprise, the boss is fired and replaced; a new company relocates to our area; or our child becomes miserable at school, and his closest friends move away so he's finally willing to relocate.

If we just have the courage to let go of the narratives and memories and accept that people and circumstances have changed, we won't immediately substitute a new set of excuses for why we can't have what we want.

Ties That Bind Energetically

If you hold on to your story even after the facts and circumstances change, you create imprints in your luminous energy field (LEF) as well as energetic cords that tie you to the players in the drama. The cords that join you to those individuals are energy filaments that can remain long after your relationships with them have changed. Shamans are able to sense these connections to the point that they can tell who's on the other side of the rope that's tied to your neck. So even if you're no longer furious at your former best friend whom you stopped speaking to years ago, you may have a cord binding you to her that keeps that relationship, and your karma with her, unresolved. It's what makes you go ballistic when you find out that she's gone and hurt someone else, or when you're reminded of an argument you had with her back when you were still friends. These cords are like feeding tubes, which you use to continue nourishing yourself with the sour milk of anger and resentment.

If you don't cut the tie to your ex-pal, you'll end up re-creating a similar situation in your life in order to find forgiveness and peace. You'll also continue to cling to the story known as "She Hurt Me, and I Am a Victim." Then each time you retell the old tale, even if it's just to yourself, you'll create new feelings of sadness, anger, and resentment, thus reinforcing what's binding you to her. (You'll also deepen the imprint in your LEF that you created in your interactions with her.) The mark in your LEF can be so strong that you need only hear your old friend's name to instantly feel enraged.

We can even remain energetically tied to other people after they die, remembering the pain they caused us instead of recalling the lessons they taught us. These types of toxic connections are very common in the West, where we hold our ancestors responsible for what's wrong with us today. These cords can keep the dead trapped between the worlds, unable to find rest or peace. They then become earthbound spirits that haunt our houses and our lives, tethered to us by our wounds.

An energy tie that binds you to someone else can drain you of vital energy, almost as if you had a parasite. It will continue to exist as long as you allow your paralyzing story to replay itself over and over again. This reminds me of a client I once had, whom I'd see once a year or so. She was constantly arguing with her mother about the men she'd get involved with, for this woman's mom believed that no man her daughter liked was ever good enough.

I hadn't seen my client in over a year when she walked into my office one day and simply announced, "The witch is finally dead," meaning that her mom had passed on several months previously. Since then my client hadn't been able to sleep properly and had become involved with three separate "bad boys," as she called them. All were men who seemed great in the first few days and weeks of the relationship but then became abusive with her.

When I scanned her LEF, I noticed that she had a huge cord attached to her heart that connected to her mother, who was unable to leave her alone even after death. (Of course my client had continued to prove her mother right!) During our session, we had to cut the cord that was binding this woman to her mom. I also asked her to thank her mother for all her love and caring, misdirected as it often was. Then she needed to tell her mother that it was okay to go home to the world of spirit, where she belonged now. Soon afterward, my client reported that she began sleeping well again. She also ceased being attracted to the "wrong" men.

If you suspect that you have an energy bond to another person that's draining you, the following exercise in forgiveness will help you free yourself of the pain and energy drain of that connection.

Exercise: Severing the Ties That Bind

While there are shamanic techniques for cutting the cords that energetically tie us to another person, we can also sever these bonds through the practice of forgiveness. This practice is a three-step process—unfortunately, most people accomplish only the first two, finding momentary relief and satisfaction, but not effectively severing the energetic and karmic ties in the LEF. It's imperative that you do *all three steps* in order to completely release yourself from the other person:

1. The first step is to identify someone who has wronged you or whom you have wronged. Take a deep breath and exhale, releasing with that breath all the anger and injustice that you may feel. Repeat this for as many breaths as you need.

2. Next, take another deep breath and blow a prayer or a blessing toward this person, forgiving them for anything they may have done to you. And then, in your mind's eye, ask them to forgive you for anything you might have done that hurt or wronged them, repeating the following to yourself: "I release you and bless you." Repeat this for as many breaths as you need.

3. The final and most important step is to contemplate the lesson that you learned from this person. What was life trying to teach you through that individual? How do you receive the lesson in its totality so that you don't ever have to learn it again? How do you turn what was once a source of anger or wounding into a source of compassion and power? It is up to you to write the new story of this relationship.

≈ ≈ ≈

Once we've discarded our old stories, cut the karmic cords, and begun to heal our wounds, we stop being consumed by the dramas of our lives and feeling stuck in a nightmare. Then we can begin to dream a far more fulfilling dream.

~~~~~~

CHAPTER THREE

Awakening into the Dreamtime

~~~~~~~~~~~~~~~~~~~~~~~~~~~~~~~~~~~~~

Logic will get you from A to B.
Imagination will take you everywhere.
— ALBERT EINSTEIN

~~~~~~~~~~~~~~~~~~~~~~~~~~~~~~~~~~~~~

The Australian Aborigines believe that two separate realities exist: that of everyday life, and that of the dreamtime, the timeless realm from which energy beings (the gods) first sung the world into existence. The dreamtime is the domain of song and poetry, of symbols and archetypes; the shamans believe that it's the more important of the two realities, for it births, shapes, and forms the physical world. They'd probably agree with Einstein, who said, "Reality is merely an illusion, albeit a very persistent one."

In our own culture, we've come to value our waking reality so much that we've forgotten our power to conceive from the invisible world of the dreamtime and co-create with the universe. The physical world can be very harsh—especially when we're faced with challenges such as disease, war, famine, and poverty—so it makes sense that we draw upon our mind to try to figure out how to solve all the problems we perceive. Yet when we don't recognize the power of the dreamtime, it's as if we become nearsighted: We can only see what's right in front of us, one tiny piece of the puzzle. We don't have the vision to take in the larger picture and begin playing with it. If we dream while we're awake, we can see that our beliefs about reality can be altered, that they're only hypotheses that are always self-fulfilling.

If your belief is *I can't master technology because it's too confusing,* or *I don't have any patience for people who don't think the way I do,* test that supposition out. Remember, the universe will inevitably prove you right. Try to remain open to the possibility that as of today, those stories can be exchanged for more interesting hypotheses.

Building a Cathedral

During the Middle Ages, two stonemasons were working in Paris on what would become the cathedral of Notre Dame. A traveler, intrigued by their activity, stopped to ask the first one what he was doing. "Squaring a stone," he replied.

"I see," said the traveler. But his curiosity was still aroused, so he walked over to the other mason and asked what he was doing.

"I'm building a cathedral," reported the man.

Just like these stonemasons, we can choose to live our story in a way that's limiting or in a way that's empowering and inspiring. This is the first step to dreaming the world into being: understanding that our actions are occurring in more than one dimension or plane. We can be certain that the man who says he's building a cathedral has a greater sense of meaning, purpose, and power than the other man who's merely squaring a stone—even though at one level of reality, both are engaged in the same activity. Building a cathedral happens in the dreamtime, while squaring a stone happens in linear, ordinary time. The Notre Dame cathedral took nearly 200 years to complete, yet in the dreamtime or the "all at once," the cathedral already existed, and the second mason in the above story could be part of a project much greater than he was.

One of my clients came to see me not too long ago complaining of depression and what he called "terminal boredom." A successful entrepreneur who had inherited a match factory that had been in his family for decades, he told me, "I want to make a difference in the world. Unfortunately, I'm stuck mass-producing matches for people to light cigarettes and get cancer."

On a superficial level, this man had everything one aspires to in life, including a fancy car, a big house on the beach, and a beautiful family. Yet he felt that he was stuck in a rut making matches and reading financial reports. He wondered if he should sell his company and perhaps develop a business venture that aligned more closely with his longing to contribute something to the world. In his mind he wasn't building a cathedral, he was engaging in tedious and meaningless labor.

I pointed out that the matches were only props in the story he'd written about himself, and cashing out was an easy way to avoid writing a new, heroic account of his life. I explained that if he couldn't find a way to change the world with matches, then he probably wouldn't be able to do it with anything else. So we began to explore that deeper dimension in which he felt a victim of his own success, a King Midas sitting before his banquet table yet unable to partake in the feast.

Matches have much potential as metaphors, so my client and I started playing with ideas such as "bringing a bit more light to the world." Eventually, he changed his story from being trapped in a golden cage while helping people get lung cancer to something much more creative. He started printing wise sayings inside his matchbooks and inspirational quotes on his matchboxes. One of my favorites invited people to "light your life on fire" with every match they struck. My client also recognized that if he wanted to change the world, he had to begin with the men and women who worked for him. Within six months he'd instituted a profit-sharing plan that made his company even more productive because it motivated his employees to put forth their best efforts.

Dreaming requires courage. You need to admit to any self-fulfilling prophecies of victimhood that you've created or bought into, let go of them, and come up with something better. In this new story, you get to play the role of a hero—not the hero who goes around rescuing damsels in distress and is knighted and celebrated, but the one who overcomes tragedy and adversity.

After all, heroes don't necessarily have trumpeters and ticker-tape parades announcing their arrival.

For example, although it's rarely heralded, parenting is a heroic act, especially now that mothers are expected to not only raise the children but also contribute income to the needs of the household. Mothers can discover their hidden powers and inspire their children by modeling for them how to live with beauty and grace. It's highly probable that mothers forge new paths and go where no one has gone before because they no longer fear the dark forest of the unknown. Confident in their power, mothers use it wisely rather than by drawing their swords and slashing away wildly at every shadow in the woods. They tend to act like courageous heroes because that's exactly what they are.

In the following exercise, you'll be retooling your core story, which has become a disempowering nightmare, and find the courage to act heroically.

Exercise: Writing the Hero's Story

As you'll recall, in each of the three key fairy tales that serve as templates for our own nightmares, the main character had to discover his or her courage and then act from it. King Midas had to humble himself to ask for help from Dionysus and give back his gift, tossing what he'd most longed for into the river. The Lion King had to face his evil uncle in order to regain his throne and bring order and health to the creatures in his kingdom. Cinderella had to have the guts to go to the ball even though she'd been told that she had no hope of being chosen by the prince to be his bride. Each character ended his or her paralyzing nightmare by taking action.

Return to the story you wrote for the exercise on page 49, in which you identified a victim, a bully, and a rescuer. Rewrite it now, casting yourself as the hero who faced a challenge, found courage, and acted. It doesn't matter whether this has actually played out in your life yet or not—once you've penned the script, you can invest yourself in it and make it come true.

To revise your story, remember that you must drop the stock characters. For instance, the father whose son was benched by his soccer coach wrote a tale about three people, and if he wants to cast himself as a hero, he needs to act creatively. He must invite the other characters of his son and the coach to become heroes as well; that is, to become individuals who access their own courage and act accordingly. It takes valor to accept not being picked for a job because you have to develop your skills further, to face the fear that you'll screw up and everyone will hate you, or to understand that you or someone you love will get their feelings hurt. So by rewriting your script, all three characters in it can wear the mantle of bravery instead of having to play out the tired roles of victim, bully, or rescuer.

When you've finished editing, close your eyes and imagine the new scene playing out in your head. (Perhaps the father would have a chat with the soccer coach, for instance, empowering him to help the man's son.) Feel the courage arising in you as you act in this new, heroic way. Enjoy the feeling of watching the other people involved access their own courage and act in alignment with it.

Now try to commit this scene to memory. You may even want to read your revised script aloud each morning, and spend a few moments envisioning and then experiencing it in your imagination. In this way, your new story can begin to manifest in the physical world.

As I said earlier, the brain doesn't distinguish between reality and imagination or memory. When you remember your feelings of powerlessness as a child, you'll re-create those feelings in the moment. But if you recall confidence or compassion, you'll create those instead. Imagining yourself successfully accomplishing a task causes your brain to lay the neural pathways for you to achieve success. So when you experience this new, courageous story playing out in your mind's eye, you'll begin training your brain to perceive your power to act bravely.

Keep in mind, however, that the dream has to be more than just a mental act to truly have power. It has to go beyond mere fantasy or idle visualization—it has to actually resonate in your heart and soul, where you can access the powerful force of your courage to act.

Dreaming Through the Power of Intent

Intent is another term for active, courageous dreaming. It is the fire of inspiration and transformation, the passion that drives us. Intent is the heart's powerful longing for the beloved, for God, for the return home to where we belong and recognize our role in the mandala of creation. Intent is the courage of the soul.

When we tap into the force of intent in our heart, the first thing we experience is peace. Many spiritual traditions say that we must strive to find this peace through prayer or meditation. (Both of these are powerful paths, and prayer and meditation are part of my personal daily practice.) We can find the "quiet place" within, where the world of doing gives way to stillness, where it ceases to be separate from the divine, and where all that exists is infinity or God. But we're not only interested in finding inner peace—we also want to bring it to the planet.

When you experience inner peace, you don't come home from protesting the war in the public square only to start harassing your partner for not stopping at the grocery store and grumbling about the thoughtlessness and incompetence of everyone around you. With the intent of peace burning like a flame in your soul, you're able to express serenity in every moment, no matter how small, even if your stomach is growling and the refrigerator is empty. You live the dream of peace and watch it manifest in your life, eagerly and naturally seizing upon the opportunities to express your inner tranquility out in the world.

Intent has tremendous power because it comes to us from the essence of the universe itself. In fact, intent is the original "juice" of creation that all but disappeared from our world after the big bang, the force that allowed our entire cosmos to emerge from a singularity no larger than the head of a pin. We can access the power of this original essence of creation to dream the world into being and consequently become great healers and visionaries. Alternately, we can be seduced by this same force and employ it for personal gain, accumulating wealth and power at the expense of other people.

Any of us can access the power of intent; what's difficult is to learn how to use it wisely. Our most terrifying dictators *and* our most beloved saints tapped into this force, calling it by its other names, such as *faith, prayer,* and *grace.* Intent is what drove Mother Teresa to begin caring for the poor of India, but it's also what allowed Adolf Hitler to envision a fatherland and a terrible wave of violence that would enable him to forge the world he imagined.

Hold the intent of peace in your heart, and you'll find it easier to express its power when you're in a challenging situation, such as when a hostile person tries to blame his or her anger on you. You'll be able to remain open to all sorts of unforeseen possibilities, to trust that you'll find the courage to operate with integrity, to be creative, and to love. Intent allows you to dream and access unseen resources so that the universe begins to actively conspire on your behalf and reflect the state of your inner peace back to you.

Will is the mechanism through which we try to force the world to conform to the way we think things should be, while intent is the mechanism by which we dream creatively and courageously. And while will corrects and fixes things after they've manifested, intent shapes things before they're even born. Both are important, but dreaming can only happen through intent.

Dreaming through intent feels very unnatural to us at first because we've been told that if we want to get something done, we'd better do it ourselves—that is, we'd better "put our minds to it" and start working. We've been told about the power of positive thinking and encouraged to recite affirmations about the exact amount of money we want to make this year or what our future romantic partners will look like. Many people swear that placing an order with the universe as if it were the Great Waitress in the Sky works, but these are often the same individuals who tend to ignore the many more times that the universe delivered a burger when they ordered filet mignon . . . or delivered the filet, but then presented them with a bill they couldn't possibly afford to pay.

On the rare occasions when willing the universe to give you what you want works, it's only because it happens to tie into a powerful intent rooted in your soul. Your soul doesn't really care what meal is on your plate or how much is in your bank account; it's far more concerned with expressing in the world the gifts you have to offer. So if your intent is one of healing, you might become the medical researcher who finally finds a cure for cancer and achieves worldwide fame, and your soul will be happy.

If that same intent simply results in your being the person everyone loves to be around because, through your example, you inspire them to be lighthearted, your soul will also be happy. You see, your soul doesn't need to take credit, and it isn't particular about exactly how the artistic act of co-creation with the universe plays out—it just wants to pick up the guitar and improvise along with divinity.

~ ~ ~

While the mind can sometimes be a helpful guide, shaping the way intent is expressed in the world, we must let the dream unfold as it will. We shouldn't work so hard at trying to figure out just how that intent might manifest.

When the shamans first took me under their wing, I probably seemed to be just another kid from America who was looking outside of his ordinary life for some insight into his personal dramas. It was the early 1970s, and I'm sure that many blue-jean clad young men and women had made their way to the ancient cities of Peru looking for an answer they were certain wasn't to be found back in Omaha or San Bernardino. However, the Earthkeepers had a dream to disseminate their teachings to the West, and they were able to see not just another searcher in me, but a potential messenger who could help them as well. They had an intent and recognized the opportunity to use me as one of their spokespeople. They perceived me to be an educated white person who interacted with other educated white people who had the ability to change a world they felt was becoming increasingly endangered. The shamans sensed that I could bring their teachings to individuals they otherwise wouldn't reach.

Yet as strong as their intent was, I wasn't sure that being a Western shaman was a task I could take on. None of my stories prepared me for this. After all, the story I told myself at the time was that I was the son of immigrants, and that my family had lost everything that was of value to us. I saw how my father, once a politically connected and important man in Cuba, was now unemployed. When I was starting out on my own career path, my attitude was, *If my father couldn't find a place for himself in this new country we're living in, then I certainly can't.*

Then when I met the Earthkeepers, I thought of myself as simply a medical anthropologist doing research for a dissertation. And after I took up the task of articulating their wisdom teachings in a contemporary, poetic manner, I had to buck my own profession and the academics who criticized me for being unscientific. (The man who was building a cathedral didn't make many friends among his fellow masons.)

In later years, my books began to be used as texts in some universities, and I helped launch an entire movement of spiritual travel to Peru. But most important, today I train other Western shamans—men and women in health care, business, and education who are bringing energy medicine to their families, to their organizations, and to the world. The possibility that I could do all of this was present when I first met the Earthkeepers, but I certainly didn't envision it all. If someone had said to me, "This is what you'll be doing in the future," I would have scoffed at this improbable outcome.

The Earthkeepers I worked with achieved their vision of finding a messenger to the Western world because they didn't micromanage it. They didn't try to figure out whom the best messenger might be, where they could find him, or how they could test him to be sure that he was better than any other candidates. They didn't think through exactly what they were going to do to spread the word about the traditions of stewardship of Mother Earth. They simply intended to deliver their wisdom to the Western world and, when opportunities for doing so appeared, they used them. Unbeknownst to me, I happened to be a walking opportunity, and the shamans recognized it because their intent was clear, unclouded by the will or the ego. They invited me to be part of a greater story than I ever could have conceived of by myself . . . yet this too is a story that I dreamed up.

Letting go of the need to control the outcome and instead serving the unfolding dream is extremely potent. For example, Nelson Mandela spent 27 years in prison, all the while focused on his intent to create a postapartheid era in South Africa. In his dream, black and white South Africans had the same opportunities and worked together to build a country in which all people could raise their children and live their lives in peace, enjoying health and prosperity. He could have dwelled on how unlikely it was that he would ever get out of prison and be able to influence his compatriots through his actions, but instead he immersed himself in the dreaming process.

I imagine that as each year passed, and then those years turned into decades, it became increasingly difficult for Mandela to hold steadfast to his dream instead of panicking or despairing. But because he had the courage to dream, he emerged from prison with tremendous strength and the power to inspire others when the moment finally came and South Africa was ready to transform.

Our Dreaming Partners

Our desire to see ourselves as iconoclasts alone in the woods causes us to forget that we're surrounded by others who would eagerly share our dream and help it come true. To that end, many men say that their favorite movie is *High Noon*, the story of a small-town sheriff in the Old West (played by Gary Cooper) who is abandoned by his community, his friends, and even his wife as he stoically awaits his opportunity to do the right thing and face down the town's enemy. No one shares the sheriff's conviction, but he holds on to it anyway.

With courage, we can let go of the egotistical need to be the lone white hat. We can put aside our shyness and come together with others to create and then manifest our dream. Remember that we can accomplish anything as long as we give up the need to take credit for it. The perception of our individuality, our separateness from the matrix of infinity, is an illusion that prevents us from accessing intent for dreaming. Our egos trip us up every time.

At the ego level, we become attached to exactly what we want, regardless of what anyone else desires. We want other people to turn away from their belief systems, embrace our values, and live their lives the way we live ours because we like to believe that would cure the world of its problems. This isn't dreaming; it's trying to force the universe to conform to the vision of one obsessed individual.

A great example of this is Paul Wolfowitz, a leading architect of the Iraq war and former president of the World Bank. Wolfowitz was consumed by the idea of wanting to save the world, first by bringing democracy to Iraq, and then by fighting corruption in Africa. Yet as he pursued these goals, he actually managed to alienate everyone he was trying to assist—especially when he helped launch the United States into what some are calling "World War III," the so-called War on Terror that would change the world's perception of the U.S. from that of a wise older brother to a bully.

Like Wolfowitz, in our arrogance we assume that we alone know what's best for everyone else, that we don't need to work well with others. But truly original dreaming begins when we're in *harmony* with other people and the world around us. Here we recognize our connection to others, but more than that, we experience it. We stop feeling like a drop of water that is separate from the ocean; our boundaries disappear as we lose sight of the point at which we end and the ocean begins. We understand that as part of that great sea, we're smoothing the edges of rock or carving a canyon, but we don't need to get a bronze plaque engraved with: THIS CANYON COURTESY OF A GENEROUS GIFT FROM _____.

In this harmony we can still retain our self-identity, our likes and dislikes, and our opinions, but they don't matter very much when we experience this feeling of oneness. Our individual concerns become secondary to the greater good. Just as the heart supports the whole body but is its own distinct entity, we can recognize and work with our gifts, talents, and skills while not puffing ourselves up with self-importance and trying to get everyone to do as we do.

∼ ∼ ∼

In order to tap into the power of dreaming, we have to be connected not only to humanity and the human story, but to all of nature and creation as well. Our sense of oneness has to include the rivers and the trees and the crickets. Our story has to become much larger, to include the stars and the galaxies. We have to sense our interconnectedness with everything in the universe so that the energies of intent can flow through us like galactic winds. As a medicine woman from the American Southwest would respond to the question of who she is, "The winds am I, the red rocks am I, that star blinking in the night sky am I."

Far too often we buy into the nightmare of iconoclasm, assuming that no one else out there can truly understand what we're going through or share our dream. Or, if we do believe that there may be others out there who can join us, we don't trust that we can find them because they're too few in number, too far away from us, or too uncommitted. This is the great disconnect: When it happens, we don't have access to the power of intent, and our dreaming becomes a mere parody of the possible, a shadow of the greatness we can experience.

We have plenty of excuses for why we can't achieve all that we wish we could have in the world, and one of the most popular is: "The problem is all those people over there. If they'd just do things my way, we wouldn't have any problems." We start to feel like unappreciated martyrs, trying so nobly to rescue the world and being sabotaged by other people.

But when we feel unappreciated and alone in our quest, like the sheriff in *High Noon* or Don Quixote, that's just another nightmare we've created for ourselves. It's extraordinary that even in this supposed Information Age, we can talk ourselves into believing that we're isolated from others who could dream with us. Many grassroots efforts these days involve men and women in different corners of the world who have never met but use technology to communicate. Even so, long before we had such technology, people found many ingenious ways to get in touch so that they could work together on their dream. The baby boomers stopped the Vietnam War without cell phones, the Internet, or text messaging. And during the Great Depression, the Okies traveled from their homes in the dust bowl to find and support one another by sharing meals, shelter, and hope.

We also tend to overthink just how a collective dream should manifest, expending enormous energy fussing over who's going to serve on what committee. Yet the Okies didn't spend time discussing Marx's theories about worker unity or contemplating the sociological and psychological aspects of collective efforts or effective communication techniques. They simply shared what food they had with others in their makeshift camps, passed along information about where there might be work, kept an eye on each other's children, and imagined a world in which they could take care of their families and find a home again.

When we set our intent and allow our courage to flow forth, we find ways to connect with other people who can share our vision; we can trust that the dream will pass from one person to the next without our having to be present at every exchange and in charge of how everything happens. In the middle of the 20th century, for instance, a newspaper publisher in Chicago printed rail schedules in his publication because he wanted to encourage African-American sharecroppers in the Deep South to move north to cities such as Chicago and create better lives for themselves working in factories. Those who employed the sharecroppers didn't appreciate this man's invitation to their dwindling workforce, so they banned the newspaper in many towns. In response, the African-American Pullman porters coordinated with people in rural Southern areas to drop bundles of the newspaper off the trains as they moved slowly through the countryside; rural sharecroppers waiting for them would then distribute the papers outside of the view of the white landowners.

Similarly, when we create an intent, people will form a chain of action without our having to coordinate it. When we dream with partners, we have to let go of our need to be recognized as the originator of the idea or the one who finally made it come true in the physical world. We may be the 117th person to get involved, unrecognized for our participation. It's only the ego that cares about whether our role was "the key one," or if anyone else knows what we did. The soul is thrilled to watch our dream become a reality and doesn't care if anyone knows what we did to help that happen.

Quantum Communication

One of the resources we have for manifesting a collective dream with our partners is quantum communication. Quantum theory shows that there are forms of exchanging information that we can't perceive with our senses yet are very real, allowing us to connect with others so that we can share and manifest empowering dreams. This kind of communication is occurring in the everyday world, not only in the subatomic realms of physics. Take, for example, a particularly clever songbird called the blue tit. Several decades ago, it made a useful discovery: By tapping its beak against the foil seal of the milk bottles sitting on doorsteps in England, it could drink the cream floating on top of the milk.

At first just a few of the birds were reported to have broken the seals, but soon blue tits all over Britain had picked up the habit, as if the information passed along instantaneously once enough of them learned how to break the seals. (This is akin to what's been called the "Hundredth Monkey Phenomenon," after an incident involving monkeys on a particular island very quickly spreading information to each other, and even to monkeys on other islands, about washing the sand off sweet potatoes before eating them.)

Due to WWII shortages, foil-sealed milk bottles were unavailable in Britain for eight years, and the generation of cream-stealing blue tits, who have a life span of only five years, gave way to a new generation unfamiliar with the bottle tops. Even so, when foil-sealed bottles were reintroduced, blue tits began breaking into them in large numbers almost immediately. It's as if their genetic memory had been altered by the previous generation's discovery.

What's more, robins have been spotted performing the same trick, but never in large numbers. It's been suggested that the birds' socialization habits are an important clue to this mystery: Robins pair off, while blue tits congregate in large flocks. Apparently, spending large amounts of time with a huge group of fellow birds allows blue tits to communicate adaptive ideas extremely quickly.

The implication for us humans is that when we isolate ourselves, it takes a long time for us to catch on to advances and new possibilities to create a different world. But if we stay connected to the larger group and regularly experience ourselves as part of the whole, we can exchange wisdom, learn, and help each other much faster.

Once when I was walking down a busy midtown street in Manhattan at rush hour, I observed a teenage boy ahead of me angrily yelling at a young woman who seemed to be his girlfriend. In an instant, the sea of well-dressed businesspeople walking uptown formed two circles: one around him, and one around her. The circle around him, made up entirely of men, had its collective chest out, either daring the boy to fight them or insisting that he settle down and conform to the rules of proper street behavior. The other circle, which was made up of women and some men, gathered around the girl with an aura of protection, and several concerned individuals asked her at once, "Are you okay?"

The movement of the crowd was as swift as a flock of birds suddenly shifting direction. No one was caught in the fear of getting hurt or thinking, *Someone—not me, of course, but someone— should do something about those two before the girl gets hurt.* Instead, as if sensing their collective power, all of the men and women acted. It was spectacular to watch, and I imagine that everyone involved felt empowered by their ability to quickly and decisively band together for the common good.

Our instinct to protect and look out for one another shines through in times of crisis, but we don't have to wait for a big, dramatic moment to feel that wonderful sense of empowerment and connection to something larger than ourselves. We can do this in the smallest of moments simply by shifting our perspective, as you'll see in the next chapter.

~~~~~

CHAPTER FOUR

Consciousness, Reality, and the Four Levels of Perception

The moment one gives close attention to anything,
even a blade of grass, it becomes a mysterious, awesome,
indescribably magnificent world in itself.
— HENRY MILLER

Our human brains experience four states of consciousness: (1) our ordinary waking one, (2) dreaming, (3) dreamless sleep, and (4) one of lucidity when we're just beginning to wake up or fall asleep. We're in one state of consciousness when we're awake, but then we slip out of it as soon as we cross the threshold to sleep. This is not so for the Earthkeepers, who are able to retain consciousness even while dreaming and can guide their dreams in any direction they desire. These men and women have mastered the art of being awake even while asleep, and they believe that most of the rest of humanity is soundly asleep even when it's wide awake.

Mastering the ability to remain conscious within these four states is essential for dreaming the lives and the world we desire. In the West we believe that the waking state is the only one in which we can experience reality. But spiritual traditions from India, Tibet, and the Americas claim that our ordinary waking state is a less-than-optimal one of awareness, one in which we become trapped in "maya" (or illusion), and they postulate the existence of superior and more favorable states of consciousness. Practices including yoga, meditation, and shamanic journeying can lead us to experience these states and even master them after extensive training and preparation. Yet the behavioral sciences believed until recently that out-of-the ordinary states of consciousness were pathological misinterpretations of reality. In fact, *psychosis* is often defined as someone perceiving a distorted reality but who doesn't recognize his or her perception as a distortion.

The state of waking consciousness that we most value is far from ideal; it actually causes us to get stuck in our mind and its illusion about the true nature of reality. This illusion is so powerful and pervasive that it obliterates all real perception and traps us in a fantastic mental dialogue from which few of us ever manage to extricate ourselves. This is the cultural nightmare that we're all educated into and only recognize when we begin to still the mind. I believe that ordinary individuals are asleep and caught in a dream that soon becomes a painful nightmare . . . which is the real psychosis. We don't recognize it because everyone around us asserts that everyday life constitutes "reality." It's only when we begin to awaken from our cultural nightmare that we recognize we've been asleep all along.

With rigorous training, we can achieve a profound vision of the inner workings of our consciousness, thus experiencing a reality that transcends our limited views of the world. This training consists of the refining of our perception, which is a practice common to yoga and meditation, as well as something you'll learn about in this chapter.

The lessons in the pages that follow are designed to help you maintain a state of lucidity regardless of whether you're awake, sleeping, or dreaming. Have you noticed how quickly your dreams fade when you're waking up? One moment you're in an absolutely real and unforgettable dreamscape, and the next you can't even recall what your dreams were about. The doorways of perception slam shut, and you're confined to only one mode of awareness. You will come to understand that there are higher states of consciousness that encompass the lower ones, where you can flow easily between the dreaming and waking realms without losing consciousness of either.

All four states of consciousness—waking, dreaming, that lucid in-between state, and dreamless sleep—are involved when we practice courageous dreaming. We experience these four states during the day, yet we're mostly unaware of them. We can be asleep while seeming to be awake; we can daydream; we can be completely lucid while driving our automobile, even as we're entranced by the piece of music we're listening to; and we can be sound asleep and dreaming vividly. The task is not to bring our ordinary waking consciousness into the dreaming state, but the other way around: to bring our dream consciousness into our waking state, where we can perceive that "life is but a dream."

Each of the four states has its particular function in dreaming the world and is associated with one of four animal archetypes of the Earthkeepers: *eagle, hummingbird, jaguar,* and *serpent.* Eagle is the state of dreamless sleep or stillness; hummingbird is the dreaming state; jaguar is that lucid state between dreaming and sleeping; and serpent is our ordinary waking awareness.

Neuroscientists understand that different regions of the brain can operate in different states of consciousness, and it's possible that we may be engaged simultaneously in all four states. Perhaps the most striking example of this is with the dolphin, in which only one half of its brain sleeps at any one time, while the other half remains awake. (A dolphin isn't able to sleep with its entire brain at once because respiration isn't an autonomic function for it as it is for us, so one half of its brain has to remain alert in order for the dolphin to continue to breathe.)

We rarely operate at our highest level of ability within any of the four levels of consciousness, and too often we operate at our lowest. So while jaguar consciousness can be lucid, logical, and coherent, it's most often muddled and riddled with unwanted thoughts and feelings. Einstein said that no problem can be solved at the same level that created it, so it's important to learn to raise our level of consciousness and master the skills and gifts within each state. To do so, we need to understand the four states of awareness that allow us to dream courageously and manifest that dream in the world. The better we understand the relationship between the brain and consciousness, the easier it will be to understand how these four levels of perception, or consciousness, work together as we operate in the world.

The Conscious Mind and the Brain

According to neuroscientists, the brain is the source of human consciousness. We know that the brain is capable of creating a simulated out-of-body experience when a particular region of the cerebral cortex is stimulated, or can even produce in us the sense of observing something at a distance. Researchers rarely consider the possibility that we might be perceiving that we're floating above our body or witnessing a distant event not because of an illusion conjured up by the brain but because such incidents actually happen. The idea that phenomena like this is the result of short circuits in our gray matter is much easier to accept.

Recent studies have led to the theory that even the belief in a god is a benign side effect of certain brain structures that evolved for survival reasons—an accident similar to the unintentional creation of beautiful columns after a series of gothic arches have been built. To a scientist, the idea that consciousness might have deliberately fashioned the brain structures needed to perceive itself seems, well, backward. Yet we know that the mind can strongly influence the very structures of the brain. For example, people who have suffered brain injuries resulting in the loss of motor function or speech have been able to create new neural connections through repetition of physical and cognitive exercises. Buddhist monks who've spent years meditating have brains that look different in a PET scan (a type of photograph of brain activity), and their brains process reality differently from those who don't meditate. Clearly we have the power to heal and influence the physical brain using our mind—but which came first, the brain or the mind?

Spiritual traditions are often at odds with science because they look at the relationship between the body, the mind, and the spirit from the opposite direction, teaching that mind or consciousness is the force that creates matter, not the other way around. According to most spiritual traditions, consciousness didn't arise out of an unintelligent primordial soup. In other words, mind did not arise out of mindless matter; rather, Spirit concocted the cosmic stew from which all life arose. Spirit fashioned an energy blueprint, which then manifested a physical reality. There was an energy blueprint for the solar system and for our galaxy and for every creature in existence. The Greeks referred to this energetic blueprint as the "Logos"; in the East it was known as the "Tao"; and some religions have called it the "world soul."

Our personal energy blueprint (or soul) is the luminous energy field (LEF) that, like our DNA, carries the stories of who we are and everything that we've experienced. But instead of storing information in chemical bonds, as DNA does, our luminous blueprint stores it as light and vibration. Perhaps better than anyone else, astrophysicists know that light carries information. In fact, the only knowledge we have about distant galaxies is through the light that reaches our telescopes across the vastness of space. The power cells for the light in our own energy field could be our very own DNA, which researchers have found emits light pulses at the rate of about 100 Hz., or 100 times per second.

The LEF is the software or set of instructions that informs our DNA, which is the hardware, to manufacture proteins that create the body. Scientists tell us that the code for our DNA is comprised of just four molecules called "bases": These are adenine (A), cytosine (C), guanine (G), and thymine (T). With these four letters, the entire poetry of creation is written. Every living thing is composed of DNA, and it is possible that DNA is the only real life form on the planet.

~~~

In the same way that DNA is the code that contains information about our genetic history and instructs our cells and tissues how to replicate, our LEF also employs a code to store information about our past. Like DNA, the LEF has four symbols that make up its code, which shamans know by their animal signs of serpent, jaguar, hummingbird, and eagle.

You might think of these four archetypal animals as representing the four layers of your LEF. These four energy layers contain imprints that can hold, for example, the story of your father telling you as a child that you wouldn't amount to anything. This information is encoded into your luminous energy field as a holographic image. Depending on the severity of this wound, it can be imprinted on the hummingbird, jaguar, and serpent layers; that is, at the level of the soul, the mind, and the body. The level of eagle is always free of personal imprints because it is the level of Spirit.

The LEF is the blueprint for the body. You can heal another (or even yourself) by removing coding in the information contained by the LEF, and the person will return to health once the energy blueprint is cleared. You do this by working from the eagle level of Spirit. Spirit existed before there was energy or matter, when all that existed was the great void—then It conceived of the universe and began to manifest the cosmos, like an artist working on a heavenly canvas that could be altered at will. In indigenous traditions, such as that of the Australian Aborigines or the Native Americans, Spirit is inseparable from the creation. Spirit is both mother and father, child and parent. Life is the art; the planets and stars and earth are the mandala; and the sky is the painting, even as it is the painter, too.

The Earthkeepers would agree with the ancient Greeks who believed that true originality and creativity come not from the human mind and biochemical reactions in gray matter, but from Spirit. The Greeks held that the Muses, the goddesses of inspiration, were responsible for all original concepts, while humans were limited to variations on the theme. So while the Muses conceived of a table as a place where people would share food communally, mere humans could only manufacture a piece of furniture and alter its basic design or function a bit.

If indeed true originality and creativity come from a source that every one of us is connected to, but that is much larger than any of us as individuals, then the process of dreaming the world actually begins in the realm of Spirit, at the level of eagle. This is where we perceive that we're a part of the Great Infinite and have the power, and even the mandate, to co-create the universe.

The Four Levels of Consciousness

We need only dream courageously and the world will arrange itself in accordance with our vision, but dreaming requires practical action at all four levels of consciousness.

You can experience peace as you sit upon a meditation cushion in your lovely garden, for instance, while someone across the street is preparing to change that. He's readying himself to come charging angrily through your gate because you set your garbage can on his lawn by mistake. This fact may not seem very important while you're in that blissful place of meditation, but at the physical level of serpent, that invasion is very real and can lead to bodily and emotional pain.

Since more than one reality exists at a time, you'll have to operate in the physical world even as you also operate at a higher level of consciousness. At a more sublime level of hummingbird awareness, you may be residing in peace, but you still have to remain aware of your environment and watch where you leave your garbage. Dealing with such concerns instead of remaining in a higher level of consciousness and letting the garbage take care of itself might appear to be hypocrisy, as if you don't trust in the power of Spirit. But if you're going to thrive in the physical world, a world that you're meant to be a part of, you must be mindful of your surroundings, even as you focus on creating peace.

Jesus referred to our need to exist in multiple realities at once when he spoke of being *in* the world but not *of* it, answering the question of whether to pay taxes to the Roman state by saying, "Render to Caesar the things that are Caesar's, and to God the things that are God's" (Mark 12:17). Put another way, God may not require a regular influx of coins, but if you don't pay your taxes, you'll be meditating on a pillow on the sidewalk.

I once had a client who had a family history of heart disease, and during a healing session I wasn't surprised to find a dark spot in his LEF, right above his heart. I explained that the doctors hadn't found any problems with his heart because the imprint in his LEF hadn't penetrated into his physical body yet, and I was able to clear the imprint. However, I warned him that he'd keep on having trouble in this area if he wasn't willing to make the lifestyle changes he needed: at the level of serpent by eating a lower-fat diet and exercising; at the level of jaguar by finding ways to reduce his emotional stress; and at the level of hummingbird by finding more meaning and satisfaction in his life. My client needed to act at all levels of consciousness in order to recover his health.

Let's explore the four levels in further detail.

Eagle Consciousness

Eagle consciousness is the highest level of perception. Brain researchers might say those in this state are experiencing predominantly *delta waves,* where the activity of their brains is so slow and quiet that it barely moves a needle on an EEG (the machine that measures brain-wave activity). Our brains produce delta waves when we enter our deepest sleep, a state in which we don't dream because we're immersed in a realm beyond words or images. This is what we consciously enter when we want to connect with the divine energy matrix, the LEF of the universe, and access its wisdom, power, and creativity. The Buddhists call this state "emptiness," and the Earthkeepers call it "the quiet place."

The eagle has the ability to soar high above a valley, visually taking in miles upon miles of terrain, yet also able to zero in on a mouse on the ground, swoop down, and capture it in his claws. The eagle is the symbol of the highest level of perception, where we're able to see the big picture and the details at the same time.

At the level of eagle, we experience that we're part of the all-seeing and all-knowing divine force.

Eagle is the domain of Spirit, of creation that has yet to manifest. When we access this state, we enter the "all at once," the timelessness in which everything exists as possibility and has the potential to spring forth into so-called reality. In eagle, we can see into the far future and the distant past, knowing things we can't know when we're in an ordinary state of consciousness.

Here we can immerse our awareness in the river of time and travel to where mussels have taken hold in a lake, consuming the phytoplankton and causing fish to die and algae to grow rampant. That is, we recognize what's happening but don't frame it as a "problem." We simply perceive all that is around us and understand how nature is interacting with herself. We recognize that we're inseparable from the mussels, the fish, the water, and the algae. In the oneness, we don't see anything to be fixed or eradicated, since all is a part of "what is." We're part of the world in all its beauty and complexity; we don't find any boundary between us, the Creator, and the amazing creation.

At the level of eagle, we can see what will happen in our future as a result of the life choices we've made. We see the death we're headed toward *and* the life we'll live as we travel along that trajectory. We don't panic or begin to plan how to change that trajectory—we simply observe, accept, and feel our oneness with the cycle of birth and death, of invention and destruction and reinvention.

In eagle, we note that the cause of our current behavior may lie in the future, where we experience the heart attack and early death that pulls us toward it along a pathway that includes consuming a high-fat, high-sugar diet and living a sedentary lifestyle. Knowing that this is our future, we can choose to retain that awareness as we return to a more embodied level of consciousness and start to feel a desire to fiddle with our portion of creation.

Hummingbird Consciousness

To support its extremely high metabolism, the hummingbird must consume huge amounts of nectar. Some species also have to store enough food and energy to make their annual migratory journey from the northern United States and Canada to South America. The hummingbird is the symbol of the great traveler, and at this level of perception, we recognize that each of us has a unique journey to take. For some of us, it will be one of great suffering; for others, it will be one of searching and discovery. But we can all enjoy a voyage of exploration and deepening, as we become more aware of our spiritual nature and the unique gifts that we can employ to dream a better, more beautiful world.

Here we're operating at the level of the heart and soul. We're not focused on finding the hundreds of flowers we must drink from in order to survive today; rather, we're concentrating on the journey we're going to take. We have the courage to embark on the seemingly impossible 500-mile flight across the ocean. We don't fear petering out somewhere over the Gulf of Mexico, worry if we've bulked up enough, or stress over where the next flower is to be found. We naturally navigate to each blossom and partake of its nectar, focusing our intent on taking the great flight to our destiny.

The perceptual state of hummingbird is associated with the soul, which is aware that Spirit is residing within us. Here we step back from protesting against war and start to conceive of what peace would look like, what part we'd play in it, and how our talents would foster this peaceful world. We step back from the "problem" of having a child with autism and instead envision what the lives of our child and all of his or her family members (including us) might look like at their finest so that we can begin to create it. We recognize that our problems are opportunities to deepen our experience of Spirit. This is the level at which intent molds and shapes reality, the place from which we access the gifts of the heart and soul, which allow us to dream courageously.

This perception is associated with *theta waves*, the activity of the brain that occurs when we're in a light sleep, dreaming, or even just fantasizing as we drive down the freeway. It's a profoundly creative state: Ideas that eluded us in our ordinary waking hours now appear to us symbolically. It's the domain in which we perceive in metaphors, and we understand why the painter chose to color one bloom in his still life white and all the others blue, without having to think through the answer.

In hummingbird, we observe what we can't sense at the level of the mind (jaguar) or the senses (serpent). We perceive perfection because we understand how different events and situations are woven together in an exquisite tapestry. For example, we see a divorce as an ending and a beginning, a source of pain and joyous freedom at the same time. Or we can watch someone die and feel profound sorrow yet also experience joy and awe as we observe the beauty of his or her passing from this realm to the next.

At this level, we can use visualization to direct our intent to organize the world. The imagery we create—the dream we allow ourselves to paint in our mind's eye—is accompanied by the certainty that it will be so, along with the delight of knowing that the vision we're creating will have a life of its own. Just as the painter approaches the canvas with an idea of what image he wants to create, but then gives in to the serendipitous discovery that a very different picture is coming forth from his brush, we can enjoy the excitement of watching our dream unfold in its own way, in its own time, surprising and delighting us.

Jaguar Consciousness

In the Amazon, the jaguar is considered the guardian and protector of the rain forest. She is the finest hunter, striking her prey quickly and altering a situation dramatically in an instant. She has no predators and lives free of fear. She is playful and curious about her world, and she plots out her hunt to ensure success. For these reasons, shamans associate the jaguar with the realm of ideas that allow us to explore, plan, and create a sudden shift in situations through changing our perspective. It's the level at which we think and feel; here our brains also experience *alpha waves,* which are associated with meditation and relaxation, lucid dreaming, and the state of awareness we experience as we're just falling asleep or waking up. We figure out ways that we might make our visions come to fruition, and we adjust our plan to keep our own passion burning while we inspire others.

Operating from jaguar helps us manifest our dreams, as we use our minds and emotions to carry out our intent. However, we have to be careful not to get stuck here—as Oscar Wilde said, "Action is the last resource of those who know not how to dream." Remember that it's our mind and emotions, and the unconscious actions that result from them, that keep us in a nightmare populated by the stock characters of victim, bully, and rescuer.

Too often we believe that our minds are so clever that we can think our way out of any problem, or we let our emotions rule and block ourselves off from other people's feelings and thoughts or even the larger picture. We become entrenched in being right and then wonder why we have so many conflicts and problems. This is what happens when we don't let our dreams organize and inform our thoughts, feelings, and actions.

Serpent Consciousness

The physical level of reality is represented by the serpent, who has no thoughts or emotions and who operates on pure instinct. It senses the grasshopper and gobbles it down without feeling mercy or thinking about what the insect's experience of death will be like. The serpent does what needs to be done—killing and digesting, slithering and resting—and doesn't plan for a journey or hunt. In this physical realm, everything is exactly as it seems to be: a stone is a stone, a threat is a threat, a meal is a meal. There is no thought, no emotion, no metaphor generated in the realm of the soul. Everything is instinctual.

Serpent can be a very helpful level of consciousness because our instincts can guide us quite well. When we're tuned into our instincts, operating with the keen awareness of the physical world as the serpent does, we can smell danger and opportunity, identify trust or fear in another, and respond accordingly. If we don't let our minds talk ourselves out of it, our intuition can help us tremendously in assessing a situation and doing what needs to be done, spontaneously.

Unfortunately, for many of us in the West, our instincts have become flawed. We trust the wrong people and push away the ones who genuinely care about us. A friend of mine, for instance, had such flawed instincts that if there was a single psychopath at a party, she'd be irresistibly attracted to him. Within moments of meeting, they'd be gazing into each other's eyes, lost in love . . . and two weeks later I'd be hearing about how Mr. Perfect was a perfect jerk.

When we're stuck at the level of serpent, there's no dream to organize our reality, nor is there even a story to make sense of our feelings—there's simply action. When a stranger shows up unexpectedly in our yard, we perceive him as a threat and act out of pure instinct. Of course to be a part of society, we have to be able to check such behavior; after all, we're expected to use common sense rather than automatically striking out at anyone who happens to wander onto our property. (Luckily, at jaguar we pass laws to regulate people's behavior and keep the peace.)

Organizing from the Top

The four levels of consciousness can be thought of as energy bodies of different frequencies, with the lightest, most quickly vibrating one enveloping and organizing the denser ones like Russian nesting dolls. Spirit's body is the matrix of the universe itself, which envelops the individual like a mother embracing her child—this is the matrix of energy associated with eagle perception. The soul is the LEF, a vibrating field of light that acts as a blueprint for our thoughts, feelings, and physical body. The LEF surrounds our mental or emotional body, and in the center of all these is the dense energy of the physical body. Spirit fashions the soul, which fashions the mind and emotions and personality, which mold the body in their own image. The body can't understand how all of this fits together, and the mind boggles at the thought that it isn't in charge of all these levels of reality.

Each of the energy bodies is inclusive of the ones within it, yet can't be described by them. Thus, the soul contains the mind and body but can't be explained by them. And at hummingbird, we're aware of all that we know at jaguar and serpent.

We can compare these to the four levels of organization in the physical body: those of cells, tissues, organs, and creatures. The cells of an eagle came together first into tissues and then formed organs, yet the cells in the stomach, the tissues in the stomach walls, and even the stomach itself know nothing about hunting—they just play their roles in the digestive process. Only the eagle understands the hunt for food. While each of its systems operates at its own level with perfection, none of the lower levels can exist if the bird doesn't hunt and eat. The eagle can't be described by its cells, tissues, or organs, yet it contains all of these. The superior levels include the ones below them but can't be defined by them. The level of consciousness must be raised to comprehend the hunt.

All four bodies of consciousness have a particular kind of awareness. At the physical level, we're concerned with the four F's: feeding, fornicating, fighting, and fleeing. Here our driving force is the unconscious thought of *I kill/screw/eat/run, therefore I am*. At the level of the mind, we're driven by the thought of *I think, therefore I am*. The soul is driven by the understanding that *I am, therefore I am*. This is the level at which we become aware of the divine within us and around us. Yahweh, the Hebrew word for *God*, essentially means "I am what I am." It's a state of being and awareness that takes us above the realm of mere thoughts, feelings, and words to one in which only poetry, metaphor, and art can capture what we experience. At the level of eagle, there is no "I" whatsoever, no individual consciousness. There is only Spirit. It is what the Persian poet Rumi referred to when he said, "I have ceased to exist, only *you* are here."

To dream courageously, we enter eagle, the realm of endless creativity and true originality, then return to the consciousness of hummingbird to marshal the tremendous force of our intent. We begin dreaming from this level of the soul—where poetry, metaphor, and vision are our palette—and open ourselves to however that dream unfolds. Using the consciousness available to us at jaguar, we find ourselves thinking and feeling in alignment with our dream, and at serpent we're compelled to act in accordance as well.

At each of these levels, we're able to access a different type of courage that can help us dream into being the lives we long to experience. Just as the four levels of consciousness are all necessary for engaging the world creatively, four types of courage make it possible for us to act in ways that truly make a difference.

~~~~~

CHAPTER FIVE

Four Kinds of Courage

*It is curious that physical courage should be
so common in the world and moral courage so rare.*
— MARK TWAIN

As a species, we humans are very intrepid. Ever since we first arrived on the planet, we've found ways to survive the elements, overcome the challenges of nature that have threatened our survival, and explore our world in order to make our lives less brutish and short. However, we have far more potential for courage than we're currently exhibiting. The difficulty is that we're usually not accessing our bravery, and even when we do, we're only drawing on the most primitive form of it. This physical form of valor is useful at times, but in the West especially, we overvalue it and overlook other forms that are far more needed today—that of Spirit (eagle courage), the soul (hummingbird courage), and the mind (jaguar courage, also known as *intellectual, moral,* or *emotional courage*).

While we're particularly in need of courage of the soul at this time in our history, all four types ultimately affect our ability to change our lives for the better because each of them is rooted in an awareness that informs our actions. With eagle consciousness, we understand why we were born into the families and lives that we have, as well as what we came into this world to learn and discover. With hummingbird awareness, we draw the soul maps to navigate through our lives, and we steel ourselves to undertake our great journey. With jaguar consciousness, we select the situations, partnerships, and endeavors that will allow us to wholeheartedly explore our soul maps. With serpent awareness, we undertake the actions and deeds that will keep us true to our journey.

This chapter will help us thoroughly examine each kind of courage so that we can tap into them when the time comes.

Eagle Courage

In eagle consciousness, we're plugged into the divine matrix, aware that we're at one with the infinite force of the universe. To be truly creative and draw inspiration from this level—that of Spirit, of genuine originality—is the highest form of courage.

Now originality doesn't mean figuring out how to build a better mousetrap; it means conceiving of a world where mice and humans live in harmony and our lives are all fulfilling, abundant, and sustainable. This can only happen when we stop perceiving mice as adversaries that are separate from our world . . . which comes to us easily when we're in eagle consciousness.

I recently read of a boy in Canada who exhibited great eagle courage. Ryan Hreljac was just six years old when he learned in school that there are people in Africa who have no access to clean water and, as a result, they often die of disease at a young age. Ryan couldn't believe that anyone would have to walk all day to get to a clean water source—so although he was only a first grader, he became determined to find a way to finance a well for an African village. He started by asking his parents if he could do chores to earn some cash, and when he brought his meager savings to a charity that builds wells in Africa, they were so impressed by his efforts that they promised to match any more money he brought in.

Newspaper stories about this bighearted child began to appear all over the world, and as more and more people heard the story, they began contributing to what became known as "Ryan's Well."

Eventually, Ryan was able to pay for his well in Africa; his charity has inspired many people to contribute to the cause, and many more villages have received wells as the result of his efforts.

So we can see that when we have courage at the level of eagle, we have a perspective that's beyond our years and experience. We don't collude in the nightmare of powerlessness but instead trust that we will find the resources we need to manifest our dream. Eagle gives us the nerve to enter the unknown and trust that possibilities will present themselves. In this state of creativity, all the filters in our mind that tell us why we can't accomplish something disappear.

This level of inspired flow is the one musicians enter when they're improvising: They exist in the same creative space, with no boundaries separating them. Without words or even body language, they instantaneously communicate with each other; without having a specific plan for how the music ought to unfold, they create a river of melody together that carries them all along. When they listen to the playback afterward, they might be surprised by how easily and naturally they moved together, much like a flock of birds. These musicians knew exactly what to play next without having had to work it out ahead of time.

Experiencing creativity at the level of eagle is what some of us call being "in the zone," or in perfect rhythm with whatever we're doing. Because we're co-creating with the divine, the sculpture leaps out of the stone that's been encasing it, our tennis match seems effortless, and so on. Eagle creativity is fresh, original, and courageous; we don't need a story to describe it because we can simply enjoy it in all of its whimsy, messiness, confusion, brilliance, and beauty.

Prometheus's Gift

To understand the type of courage that comes from the level of eagle, it's helpful to consider the story of Prometheus, the Greek god of inspiration, craft, and creativity. According to the myth,

95

Prometheus was a Titan, a giant born of the gods. However, he had great sympathy for human beings because he'd co-created them with the help of Zeus himself. Prometheus observed humans shivering in the cold and leading short, difficult lives, and he felt sorry for them. He knew that if people could have the gift of fire, which the gods kept for themselves on Mount Olympus, they could experience warmth and cooked food; they could also use it to see in the nighttime and to heat metal and forge tools. Symbolically, the fire that Prometheus wanted to bring to humanity represents creativity and inspiration, for it transforms and illuminates. It is what allows us to dream with originality.

Prometheus stole fire from the hearth of the gods and bestowed it upon humankind, angering Zeus. While the king of the gods couldn't take fire away from human beings, he could punish Prometheus for his defiance. Thus he chained Prometheus to a rock, where he'd have his liver pecked away by an eagle every day, only to have it grow back each night so that the torture could continue. Poor Prometheus suffered this fate until many years later when Hercules, the son of Zeus, came along and freed him.

Prometheus brought humanity another great gift—the courage to defy the gods, the ability to think original thoughts and to create—and this brash act was what really caused him to be so severely punished. In the Greek myths, the gods are the only creators, and when mortals wander into their territory, it's tantamount to stealing some of their power to create and attempting to become as gods. Other patriarchal religions have taken this same attitude toward humans who encroach on God's domain: For example, Adam and Eve, who dared to know good and evil, were banished from the idyllic Garden of Eden and punished by God. But this act of defiance launched humans into our true journey, forcing us to mature and develop discernment.

The Power of Creativity

From the consciousness of eagle, we're able to mine the creativity that stretches unimaginably far beyond the limitations of our mind and its inventive powers. When our ingenuity gives us increased power over life and death, for instance, many say that we're "playing God" by daring to grow stem cells or repair DNA—as if the divine doesn't want us messing with its artistry. Eagle allows us to challenge the petty, jealous little deities our mind creates through its limitations; any act of true creativity, then, is a revolutionary act that frees us from those angry deities.

In our daily lives, our creativity defies the gods our culture worships and fears: those of greed, patriotism, conformity, prestige, and so on. We unwittingly pay homage to these gods and submit to their tyranny when we're lost in our nightmare—but when we thumb our noses at them by living creatively, everyone becomes very uncomfortable.

Not long ago, a homeowners' association was in an uproar because someone under its jurisdiction had hung a wreath shaped like a peace sign on his door during the Christmas season. Was this a symbol honoring the Prince of Peace or an antiwar statement that violated one of the association's rules about political displays? The hoopla became a national news story as people argued about the meaning of the wreath and what the "god" of the association should do.

All great creators were shunned by the gods of their day who feared originality and thought they knew best. After graduating from college, for example, Albert Einstein couldn't find work at any university because his professors wouldn't write him letters of recommendation. It turns out that they were still irritated that he'd skipped their lectures in order to do independent work that was far more advanced than what they were teaching. He got a few odd jobs tutoring children before finally landing a job at a patent office.

Vincent van Gogh was told by his brother, Theo, that the reason his paintings weren't selling in Paris was that they were too dark and somber compared to the paintings of the highly popular Impressionists. And when Johnny Depp first crafted the character of Captain Jack Sparrow for the movie *Pirates of the Carribean: The Curse of the Black Pearl,* he was called up by panicky film executives who demanded to know what he was doing—they thought that his portrayal was bizarre and he was ruining the movie. Yet the movie went on to become such a blockbuster that it spawned two sequels, and Depp's performance in that first picture earned him an Academy Award nomination.

We're often unable to recognize creative genius and great talent in our culture, be it in artists or scientists, and we treat them as a threat to our organizations. It's not uncommon in scientific circles to hear how it's easier to get funding to study the reproductive habits of a fruit fly than for original research in which there's a high probability of failure. No one wants to take the risk of losing face just to be creative; after all, such individuals have to defy the gods of academia, public opinion, and accepted "taste." Creators often suffer punishment for breaking the old rules, just as Prometheus did—Galileo was sentenced to house arrest by the Catholic Church for suggesting that the earth spins around the sun, and van Gogh only sold one painting in his entire life and ended up fatally shooting himself in the chest after having to declare bankruptcy.

When we worship the jealous, petty, tyrannical gods of our culture, we become unoriginal and closed off to fresh ideas. If we have eagle courage and embrace originality, however, we imagine a world in which there are no hard-and-fast rules about what constitutes great art; we delight in what's unusual, quirky, and unexpected; and what our neighbors display on their doors doesn't matter to us one way or another.

The creative individual is a master of courage, the person in the crowd who proclaims that "the emperor has no clothes" when everyone else is afraid to speak up. She can do this because she's true to herself and her dream, and she has no fear. She may not be a dancer or a poet, but she lives her life as an artist, surrendering to the power of creativity, seeing beauty everywhere.

Too many of us have forgotten how to be creative like we used to be as children. In the story of the emperor who wore no clothes, it's a child who points out the royal leader's nudity, speaking the truth without fear. Kids hardly know fear at all—they haven't yet learned to recognize the gods of greed, prestige, and conformity. That's why they shrug their shoulders when someone questions their choice to wear rain boots and a pink tulle skirt on a hot summer day. They don't let their rational minds or their worries get in the way of their imagination. When Jesus said that to enter the kingdom of heaven we must become like children, he was clueing us in to our need to open ourselves to divine inventiveness and inspiration if we're to experience fulfillment, joy, and heaven.

Being creative requires that you let go of that big bucket of cold water you throw on yourself and your ideas whenever things start to become really interesting. You need to stop asking yourself, "Will anyone be offended?" and "Who am I to ask questions?" and instead inquire, "What if?" What might life look like if you weren't married—or if you weren't married to your image of yourself as the powerful, independent woman who doesn't need a man? What might your relationship with your body look like if you stopped measuring, comparing, worrying, feeling guilty, and obsessing over its state of beauty? You don't have to shave your head, don sackcloth, and change your name as if you were entering a monastery, but you *can* let go of the strict ideas you have about who you are, how you want people to perceive you, and what your life is supposed to be like.

This reminds me of a successful entrepreneur I know who decided in his 60s that he wanted to become an artist. He left his business and moved to an island in the Mediterranean where "the light was just right" to paint. Although he hadn't taken up a brush since he was in elementary school, he bought an easel and oil paints and began to let the empty canvas teach him. At first he simply doodled and scratched at the fabric. But as the weeks went by, he discovered that he had entire landscapes inside of him, and these began to flow onto his canvas.

A few years later this man's art was being exhibited in galleries throughout Europe. Yet even today, when I ask him if he simply had a great talent that was waiting to emerge, he responds that he has no "talent," only a great love for what he does. He says that he follows no form or technique—he simply allows the brush to lead him in a dance across the canvas, and he's never been happier.

Hummingbird Courage

In hummingbird consciousness, we engage life from the level of the soul. Just as that tiny bird finds the valor to take his monumental journey, we can discover the courage to perceive our own lives as a journey of growth and discovery, of spiritual maturation. We don't fuss about the details of our flight because we feel confident that regardless of what the weather is over North Carolina or how few resting spots there will be as we travel across the Gulf of Mexico, we'll make it to our destination.

The hummingbird isn't even supposed to be able to fly given the shape and weight of his body. Likewise, some of us feel that we weren't made to soar through the air; we're certain that we were designed to trudge through the mud or wade through the swamp. But despite thinking that we don't have enough time, enough money, or enough "wings," we each have a great journey that's available to us should we choose to accept the invitation from life and respond to the call.

It can be very difficult to let go of our everyday worries and allow the courage of the soul to arise within. Our habit is to perceive problems in our lives and then think and work harder in order to solve them and create happiness for ourselves. As my shaman mentor once told me, "Alberto, you're always rearranging your sand castles on the edge of the lagoon that is your life." He was comparing my life to one of the oxbow lakes in the Amazon, all of which seem separate and independent but are in reality all fed by the mighty Amazon River. He went on to say, "And then there is a surge of water from the mountaintops, the river rises, and it washes away all of your dreams and plans. If you want to change your life, you have to travel upstream. There, you could divert the water easily with only the palm of your hand."

He was right—I was constantly rearranging the situations in my life, thinking that the right job or partner would "fix" all my unhappiness. If that didn't work, I'd put my efforts into explaining why I couldn't create happiness: My spouse wasn't supportive of me; my peers didn't acknowledge me; I had low self-esteem left over from my childhood. I created a lengthy list of reasons why I was miserable. In my vain attempts to fix things at the level of jaguar, I didn't understand that I indeed had the power to create happiness, but I had to do it from farther upstream. Only then could I free myself from the endless work of trying to fix my life and overcome that exhaustive list. I needed to dream courageously from the level of hummingbird so that I could begin to manifest my dream naturally and easily, without all the "efforting" I'd been doing.

Recently, a client was telling me about a wonderful man she met. The first night they spent together, she told him the long, drawn-out story of her last lover in order to explain why she was fearful of becoming intimate. She was surprised when, at the end of her tale, he jumped out of bed and left with a hurried good-bye. She never heard from him again.

Understandably, this woman wanted to establish safety for herself at each step of the dance of intimacy; however, my suggestion was that she choose the right man before ending up in her bedroom at all. I didn't mean she had to choose *the* right man, as if there were only one, but that she choose someone she could trust so that she wouldn't have to concentrate on her need for safety. Instead, she could just surrender to the risky experience of discovering love as if for the first time.

≈≈≈

Hummingbird courage can empower us to rewrite our stories to be mythical ones of heroism. Looking at life as a journey of discovery and growth—and ourselves as determined hummingbirds willing to trust that we'll have all we need on our journey—we start to paint a very different picture of who we are and what the events of our existence mean. At this level we find the courage to be the dreamweaver. Thus the story of a failure can become one of rebirth and rediscovery; the saga of a loss or illness can now be one of initiation into the tribe of survivors who can wisely guide others through this passage. Even when we're suffering greatly, we can access hummingbird courage and begin to tell a tale that eases our pain and reminds us of our resilience.

Americans have a lot of experience in dreaming at the level of soul: We dreamed of civil rights, equal rights for women, and free public schooling for all; and our Constitution and Declaration of Independence are wonderful descriptions of courageous dreams of the soul. Yes, our actions have often needed correction to be in alignment with these dreams, but again and again we've come back to them. One of the reasons why the civil rights movement gained such momentum—and inspired so many to risk their reputations and even their lives to get involved—is because when faced with the reality of incredible unfairness, people who truly held the intent of freedom and justice for all in their heart could see that the old laws and treatment of African Americans were definitely not in sync with the collective dream. Consequently, those in the movement found the courage to realign their thoughts, feelings, and behavior; and then they acted.

At hummingbird, we can rewrite both our personal and cultural stories. For instance, we don't have to pen stories of wars: the war on drugs, the war on terror, or the war on poverty. Instead, we can envision a collective ecology that renders chemical intoxication obsolete, or we can focus on healing the conditions that create the hunger that leads to violence. We could dream a garden of abundance growing in every corner of the world.

Muhammad Yunus, winner of the 2006 Nobel Peace Prize and founder of the Grameen Bank, is one of the originators of microfinancing. Rather than embracing the disempowering story that there will always be poverty, he envisioned helping individual women by investing money in their enterprises. His bank loaned small amounts, sometimes as little as $100, to women in developing nations because he believed that by doing so, he'd be watering the seeds of abundance that they already possessed.

What Yunus and other microfinanciers discovered is that despite abject poverty, the women who benefit from such loans pay them back at a rate of nearly 100 percent. They use their money not only to help themselves and their own children, but to employ other women as well. These newly empowered females recognize that by repaying their loans they're helping others like them to rise out of poverty, too.

Hummingbird courage requires doing away with the old symbolic set that we've internalized and coming up with a new one. What would our new set of symbols look like? We need to take pencil and paper to it, doodle, and find the signs of transformation that emerge from the sketching. Symbols can appear in dreams and during reverie; they may also be supplied by a healer when she gives a client a stone and asks her to carry it in her pocket and rub her hand and fingers over it.

For any symbol to have meaning, however, it must spring from the heart, not the mind. Who we are is mirrored back to us and announced to the world by the symbols we surround ourselves with. The kind of glasses we wear, the style of shoes we buy, how we decorate our homes, and even the way we walk and grimace is part of a symbolic set that states, "This is me." When we're in the process of changing, it's common to want to clear the clutter out of our closets, to change our look, to move to a new apartment or town . . . but we have to do more than superficial alterations.

In other words, a divorced woman would have to understand the symbolic importance of donating her wedding dress to the local Goodwill store. Simply tossing it out without allowing herself to feel what it means to say good-bye to that symbol isn't going to help her close the book on that chapter of her life. The lost dream, the person she was . . . all that her wedding dress represented will remain in the closet of her psyche even after the garment itself is gone. Engaging in symbolic acts at the level of hummingbird shifts the quality and energetic vibration of her luminous energy field and allows her to heal.

It takes great soul courage to perceive that letting go of an old dream isn't a concession to failure but a brave act of giving birth to a new self.

Jaguar Courage

In jaguar consciousness, we can access another very useful type of courage, that of the mind and emotions. This is sometimes called "moral courage," and it's what allows us to speak up about what we believe is right and just to people who aren't receptive to our beliefs. Moral courage dares us to risk rejection and ridicule and often contradicts mere physical bravery, which helps us do what we need to do in order to survive. With moral courage, we may actually gamble our own safety to act in alignment with our deepest held beliefs. This is the valor that firefighters draw upon when they rush into a burning building when their instincts are telling them to stay away; and it keeps lovers true to each other when things aren't going well, instead of looking for ways to bail out of the relationship.

Moral courage requires that we be willing to admit to our failings and neuroses. If we're obsessive or demanding, we acknowledge the upside of those qualities as well as the downside and try to be aware of how they both serve and hinder us. We're able to experience our emotions even as we put them in perspective. After being betrayed by someone, for instance, we acknowledge that it's normal to want to make them suffer for what they did, but we also factor in common sense and an understanding of why it's best to let go of anger and move on. Moral courage allows us to weigh both sides of the issue and recognize that other people's behavior is usually the result of their own psychological issues and obsession with their feelings—it's not that they want to hurt us but that we get in the way of their dramas.

When we lack jaguar courage, we focus only on our own survival, and compassion eludes us. We don't care what anyone else's problem is, we just want to make sure that we're not suffering. But when we're at the level of jaguar, we do the right thing regardless of the risk or cost. Such courage is what drove New Yorkers to let go of their own fears on 9/11 and seize their opportunities to help each other: whether it was the man who carried his disabled co-worker down dozens of flights of smoke-filled stairs toward safety; the merchants in Chinatown freely giving away slippers to women in high heels who had to walk miles to get home; or the bicycle-shop owner who loaned out all his rental bikes to strangers who needed to get home, asking them to just return the cycles whenever it was convenient for them. Worries about personal safety or business profits got pushed aside on that day thanks to jaguar courage.

This level also gives us emotional courage. For example, some of us can remain married for years yet never achieve true intimacy, sharing only tasks, sex, and finances. With emotional courage, we disclose our hopes and dreams to our partners, as well as our vulnerabilities and self-judgments, and open ourselves up to *being* love instead of being *in* love. Often, our fear of not being in control holds us back from being honest about our emotions and creating a new story that we can invite our partners to participate in.

And jaguar lets us enjoy intellectual courage, too. This is what scientists draw upon when they let go of the current dogma and theory and explore new possibilities—from Galileo exploring the relationship of the planets to the sun regardless of the teachings of the Catholic Church in the Middle Ages, to a scientist today insisting that he's not crazy to be studying nonlocality (the ability to influence events at a distance). Jaguar courage allows anyone to incorporate new information into his or her worldview, regardless of if it's a new scientific discovery or something a man just learned about his romantic partner that contradicts his long-held view of her.

One of my favorite quotes is the following, taken from a lecture delivered by the Nobel Prize–winning physicist Richard Feynman: "It is my task to convince you *not* to turn away because you don't understand it. You see, my physics students don't understand it either. That is because *I* don't understand it. Nobody does." Said another way, it's easy to become attached to our own preconceptions. Even Einstein said that the early work on quantum mechanics seemed like a "system of delusions of an exceedingly intelligent paranoiac." But when we're in a state of jaguar courage, we break out of the old ways of thinking and try to look at situations differently.

~ ~ ~

Creative artists have a wonderful ability to let go of judgments and open themselves up to using the "wrong" color or composing in the "wrong" genre. Ray Charles, one of the most talented musical artists of our time, often frustrated his record company by creating music in a new style instead of the one they were used to (which they knew how to package and sell to a select market). The executives would groan when he'd come in with a handful of country-blues songs or R & B tunes instead of what they were expecting, but Charles refused to be pigeonholed and go with what everyone believed worked. As a result, he was able to bring forth truly original works of art.

In our own lives, we lose our ability to break the rules and be creative very quickly when we enter our teenage years and become anxious about conforming to our peer group. Curiously, it's that drive to conform that makes us want to be "unique" among the masses, even as we dress, talk, and walk like everyone else does. *Uniquely yours* and *The unique you* are terms that are used by marketing people to sell us everything that we feel will make us stand out from the people next door. Our lack of jaguar courage causes us to forget our childlike ability to wonder, dream, enjoy absurdity, and be inventive.

I remember when I was a child, and the neighborhood kids and I used to make some of our own toys, which were often much more fun to play with than the trucks or cowboy figures my mother would buy for me for Christmas. In fact, the one I remember most fondly was a simple hoop fashioned from a broken bicycle wheel, which I'd roll along the road, guiding it with a stick.

From the point of view of jaguar, our drive to be unique results in living a life of cowardice. The jungle cat insists that we recognize our sameness, that we're all on this earth together and are brothers and sisters. Only when we recognize that we aren't special can we truly become original: We can have the courage to look at what everyone else is looking at and think something different about it.

Jaguar consciousness can bring us back to a state of openness and eagerness, but it takes courage to act on our creativity and not simply sit and ponder what our lives might be like if we had the audacity to manifest our vision. Without courage, we can become lost in fantasy, posturing and talking about all the great things we aspire to be or do but never following through on our plans. Yes, we can spin dreams, but if they're not informed by the soul, they can easily transform into nightmares. We need hummingbird consciousness to recognize that our jaguar-level dreams are limited by the perceptions of our mind and the strong emotions that can dominate our thinking.

Here's an example. The wish to become a rock star, which was rooted in a need to have pretty girls batting their eyelashes at you, becomes the ambition to own a collection of expensive, collectible guitars to hang on the wall and show off to your friends—and you never own quite enough to feel like a rock star. With the courage of the heart, you realize that running an organization with originality and compassion or parenting your child with honesty and integrity is just as "rock and roll" as tearing through a solo in front of screaming fans. You trade in false bravado for true bravery and empty symbols of rebellion for genuine revolution.

Jaguar courage, then, requires that we understand the limited perceptions created by our thoughts and feelings and be vigilant about getting caught up in dreams that are actually nightmares.

Serpent Courage

Serpent consciousness is much lauded by our culture. Our practical "can do," "tough love" attitude; our insistence on "calling a spade a spade" and "telling it like it is"; our demand for an answer to the question "Are you with us or against us?" as if those were the only options—all come from serpent consciousness. Here we identify a problem, do what we have to do, and achieve our directive . . . period, end of discussion, no need for looking more closely.

We've been taught that the type of physical courage that arises from serpent consciousness—the resolve to do what needs to be done in order to survive—is what made the United States great.

Back in our school days, we were taught that our country was founded by men and women who boldly set out to conquer the frontier: They tamed the prairies and swamps and cleared the forests that stood in their way, stopping only to shoot a charging bobcat or dangerous Indian. Mesmerized by such tales, we took pride in the thought that our veins throb with the pulsating blood of bold pioneers who could settle any land. It was comforting to think that we'd inherited such an impressive legacy of bravery.

Unfortunately, as we've discovered, this is a false legacy. It's true that the pioneers had physical courage, for they risked their lives to manifest the vision they had for themselves, and that served them well. However, they often weren't the noble iconoclasts they've been painted to be in John Wayne movies. The pioneers were very much dependent on each other; the federal government (which cleared the land of the Native Americans who occupied it); cheap immigrant labor; and, quite often, slaves to accomplish their homesteading and empire building. Most didn't have enough higher-level courage to stop thinking about their own survival long enough to dream of a world in which everyone could feel prosperous and happy without someone else having to foot the bill by giving up their land or toiling in grueling physical labor.

We've also been told to find inspiration in the ever-popular rags-to-riches story, such as the type penned by Horatio Alger in the 19th century. A typical Alger hero is the poor yet determined boy who draws on his physical courage to spend hours on the street corner, yelling "Papers for sale!" until he's hoarse. He ultimately gets a better job, working long hours to achieve the security of a big house and middle-class respectability. Such a young man succeeds because he's willing to put his poverty-stricken past behind him, believe in the American dream, and be reborn into a new life.

This archetype continues to be a part of our culture: We eat up stories about millionaires who have created success out of nothing, overcome all their psychological baggage, and reinvented themselves. We dearly want to believe that anyone—no matter what their background may be—can achieve prosperity, forget about having to struggle to survive, and live happily ever after simply by choosing to pull themselves up by their bootstraps like those young heroes of the Horatio Alger novels.

Alas, these sorts of dreams almost always turn into nightmares as the wounds of our past sabotage our success. Our physical courage might manifest wealth or reputation, but what we create is as delicate and impermanent as a sand castle on the beach. Like many of the pioneers or Alger heroes, we don't access higher forms of valor that would allow us to dream something more fulfilling for ourselves and our world. Instead, we settle for the false security of money, power, and position.

With moral courage, we can stand up for those who are being mistreated or left out of the American dream. Emotional courage allows us to be honest with ourselves and others, to live with integrity instead of slipping into a nightmare of merely trying to survive and compromising ourselves to do so. Intellectual courage allows us to question the status quo, reject dogmatic thinking, and insist on creativity— even when others are afraid of our originality.

Hummingbird courage allows us to direct our intent to be in sync with our dream. With that of eagle, we open ourselves to the truly innovative ideas that flow through us from Spirit. Yet serpent courage also has its place in the act of dreaming, even today when feeding our family doesn't require going out into a blizzard to find the barn and milk the cow. A big part of bringing a dream to life is doing the physical, instinctual work required to make it happen. But serpent courage must be informed and guided by the higher forms of bravery.

One of my clients, for instance, had a dream for a better life for her family, far away from their present Manhattan home. She longed for a sense of community, more physical space, and a closer relationship to nature; she imagined herself in a place where she could create all of this without having to struggle so hard to make a living. This was her dream at the level of hummingbird.

She and her husband worked at the level of jaguar to figure out how they could transfer their jobs to the new location. They remained in this level to choose a new home that they felt would suit their needs and to plan their move—that is, to find the boxes, pick up the masking tape, and plan the good-bye parties—while dealing honestly with their mixed emotions about the transition.

Yet when the time came for the actual move, they realized they had far more possessions than they could pack up in time to make their deadline to get out of town and meet their unpacking crew at the other end. So after exhausting the possibilities of getting more help, they entered into serpent consciousness and simply allowed instinct to take over. They pushed their bodies to pack, stack, and load the boxes via assembly line into the truck. For hours they stopped only to pay attention to their muscles' need to rest or to take short breaks as necessary.

Serpent courage means following through and getting the job done. By not working at the level of jaguar, my client and her husband didn't panic about their situation or push themselves beyond their bodies' limits, nor did they waste time venting about what a disastrous situation they were in. By staying in serpent, they were able to do everything they needed to do in time to manifest their dream.

～～～

Just as each of our energy bodies encases the ones within it, and each of the four levels of consciousness incorporates the others, the highest forms of courage encompass those that are below it. So you can't have the courage of Spirit (or even that of the heart and soul) and dream courageously if you're lacking moral, intellectual, emotional, and physical valor. They all operate together. When you truly have the courage to dream, you have the courage to act as well.

In the next part of the book, you'll learn how to use the four levels of consciousness and courage to continue dreaming each day and each moment, regardless of your circumstances.

～～～～～

PART II

From Dreaming to
Courageous Action

CHAPTER SIX

Courage as Action

> *Courage doesn't always roar. Sometimes*
> *courage is the quiet voice at the end of*
> *the day saying, "I will try again tomorrow."*
> — MARY ANNE RADMACHER

At a pivotal moment in the movie *The Wizard of Oz*, the Cowardly Lion, who has struggled to discover his courage, boldly confronts the intimidating Wizard and exposes that the supposedly "great and powerful Oz" is really just a powerless, dishonest little man. Despite his clear act of bravery—and the realization that the one he most fears is someone more nervous than he is—the Lion doesn't truly believe he's courageous until the Wizard presents him with an impressive medal of service.

Like the Cowardly Lion, we also engage in courageous acts but tend to overlook or dismiss them when they're not accompanied by the loud roar of approval and appreciation from others. With little validation for our actions, we start to believe that we aren't so brave after all. At that moment, the universe begins to mirror back to us a reality of cowardice, so our valor is unlikely to be repeated.

Most of us think of courageous acts as those that people perform when there's an obvious opportunity to step in and save the day, such as when there's an accident and someone needs assistance, but there are daily opportunities to act with courage as well. There are times when it's important to speak an uncomfortable truth that needs to be aired, for instance, or occasions when we must find the strength to break with tradition and act creatively despite our unease and the potential for protests, accusations, and recriminations from others. Such courageous deeds allow us to dream a different reality, but we tend to underestimate how important those acts are and quickly brush them aside.

If you've ever been the whistle-blower, the one who stood up to a bully, or the one who defied the norm by being true to yourself instead of caving in to others' expectations, you may have resented and been hurt by the lack of applause and support you received. With no medal of honor or public praise, you may have eventually convinced yourself that your act didn't matter all that much . . . but it did.

Limited ideas about courage being something grand and dramatic that will save the world and inspire ticker-tape parades have prevented you from recognizing that in everyday life, you can engage in empowering acts that make a very real difference in the world. Maybe you recently said to your partner, "I'm sorry—when you got angry at me, I lashed out because I was feeling defensive"; you thought, *I could cut this person down with a smart remark, but I'm not going to,* choosing instead to invite him or her to engage in a different dialogue than one of conflict; or set aside your fear of disapproval and insisted that the group you belong to rethink the grand plan to solve a problem that they're panicking about. Well, these seemingly minor actions that draw upon passion, integrity, and creativity are far more important than you've been led to believe.

Obviously it won't help to go overboard with self-congratulations and continue reliving the glory of one daring act we engaged in way back in our college days. But it's very important that each of us acknowledge and value *all* acts of courage, however small, for they create extraordinary satisfaction and motivate us to continue acting fearlessly. Only when we recognize that we've risen to our full height and exercised our humanity in a noble way are we able to experience genuine fulfillment.

It turns out that many of us claim to be on a spiritual quest, but often what we're really seeking is a warm, fuzzy feeling in our tummy that will give us a sense of comfort and make us believe that we're good people. Achieving this kind of satisfaction does feel good, but such a quest doesn't require great courage or serve anyone but ourselves. Courage isn't something to aspire to or wish for, another item to add to the spiritual résumé we use to impress other people (or ourselves). Rather, it's something to engage in daily, even hourly, regardless of whether anyone applauds us or even notices us.

It's never productive to look outside of yourself for validation of your courage, since that will take you away from achieving eagle and hummingbird consciousness. It locks you into a story of victimhood, titled "Nobody Appreciates Me." So forget the kudos from the crowd, and validate your actions yourself. Take the time to savor the sense of joy, pride, and power you create in these small moments. Then let go of those thoughts and feelings so that you're ready for the next opportunity to exercise courage.

When a basketball player makes a shot, he claps his hands, feels great, and immediately looks at where the ball is now, seeking out his next opportunity to score or help a teammate. If he doesn't move on quickly, the joy over his accomplishment will disappear instantaneously when he sees the other team rush to their side of the court and score.

Keep your eye on the ball, keep playing the game, and be open to what happens next rather than losing yourself in your reverie about your bravery. By doing so, you'll be dreaming courageously instead of getting caught up in the ego's desire for the security of reputation.

Acknowledge Unsung Heroes

Even when we do acknowledge courageous and creative deeds, we tend to focus on one person and give him or her all the credit, forgetting that such acts usually arise when someone has been supported and encouraged by others. Our individualistic values blind us to the team standing behind our icon of bravery: For example, we remember Anne Frank, but do we recall the names of those who kept her hidden in the secret annex, bringing food, news, and hope at the risk of their own lives? How many of us think about what Mother Teresa's own mother must have done to raise a daughter who had such a deep sense of compassion or ponder what the other volunteers at the saintly nun's shelter for the dying have continued to do every day now that she's gone?

Because our culture doesn't acknowledge the whole team—and we all do desire validation, acceptance, and praise—we'll often jockey for position, hoping to get the credit for any collective act of courage. So if our bravery has been overlooked, we must let go of any need to be honored by others. And it gets us nowhere to join in the culture's lack of appreciation for unsung heroes by not giving credit to anyone else, insisting, "Well, no one ever tells me I'm brave, so why should I make a big deal about what someone else does?"

Every day, all around us, people are dreaming courageously as they go about their business quietly. We overlook the courage of our co-worker who volunteers at a local boys' camp even while he's juggling the needs of his aging mother. We grumble about the cops when one of them pulls us over for a benign moving violation, but forget that the very same officer might be someone who's creating a rapport with the troubled young people in the neighborhood in the hopes of keeping them from turning to crime.

The obituaries are full of stories of neighbors we never knew who traveled the country singing and playing piano for wounded soldiers during World War II, or who led support groups for other parents who lost a young child. It can be amazing to discover just who was living down the street, making a difference in people's lives without our having any idea of their valor. When we slow down and look around us, we might be surprised at the gallant activities we're completely unaware of or know about but have always taken for granted.

When we're the beneficiaries of others' courageous acts, we may well be grateful, but it's easy to forget to acknowledge them. Saying, "Speaking up really took guts—I applaud you," "I salute you for taking the high road and not engaging in that battle," or "I really admire what you did for Dad; I know how hard it was for you to stand up for him and get him the help he needs" cultivates courage in others.

So when you spot your partner parenting your child well, express gratitude and praise. If it's your ex, let go of the story called "That Jerk Never Appreciated Our Kids" or the cynical thought of *Well, it's about time . . . although I'm sure this behavior won't last.* Instead, step into the new dream and participate in it. There are opportunities each day to celebrate courage and creativity and then manifest them. Support others with praise and offers to help out their efforts, and you'll see that people will begin to encourage you, too. And try to value and engage in genuine praise that's not motivated by a need to manipulate others or generate a return. In other words, when you see someone act with courage, pause in your busy life and allow yourself to experience joy at this display of bravery and integrity—then be sure to acknowledge what they've done.

If we fall into the bad habit of dismissing courageous acts, we become caught in our stories at the level of jaguar and in our fears at the level of serpent. By dreaming from the realm of the soul, we'll find ourselves naturally seizing upon our opportunities for courage and action.

Know That Dreams Are Not Goals

The dreams you craft at the level of the soul are very different from goals, which are tangible, measurable, and set in the future. Jaguar consciousness will help you to create specific aims, such as, "I'd like to go back to school and finish my degree three years from now," or "I want to become a published poet." A dream, on the other hand, would be something like, "I will continue to learn my entire life; let go of any rigid, dogmatic beliefs; and parent my children well," or "I will write poetry and live the life of a poet, seeing beauty all around me."

When you dream, you have a chance every day to manifest that vision through your actions. Goals will then suggest themselves, and you'll be flexible about how and when you achieve them, rather than insisting that you can't feel good about yourself until your poems have been published or you receive your diploma.

When you dream courageously, you'll find that your goals are secondary—what's most important to you is how you live today. You'll celebrate the milestones you reach and make plans, but you won't obsess about reaching a particular end point. You'll keep in mind that dreaming is about the journey, not the destination. As you tap into your soul's courage, you'll naturally start performing the actions you need to manifest your vision. Moral, intellectual, emotional, or physical courage will be there for you; you'll step into your dream as easily as you do your shoes, and you'll walk that dream right out of the door of your mind in order to manifest it.

Let's say that you're tired of feeling fatigued and unhealthy, so you decide that you want to change the way you treat your body. If you remain at the level of jaguar, you'll create specific goals of weight loss and exercise. You'll marshal your willpower and become determined to reach a particular number on the scale, vow to go to the gym and work out for 40 minutes three times a week, or swear off sugar and white flour. You'll agonize over the slice of birthday cake presented to you at your child's party and feel guilty if you don't get off the couch and work out . . . and then try to alleviate that feeling by indulging in a big helping of comfort food. Whenever you notice that you're not making progress toward your goals, you'll fault yourself and try to recover your willpower to try again.

Now if you install your dream at the level of hummingbird, you'll establish the intent to experience a healthy body, and your LEF will begin to vibrate wellness. Your emotions, thoughts, and actions will start to line up with your intent. You'll discover that you're enthusiastic about exercise class, in touch with your body, and attracted to fresh foods instead of fast meals. If you stop to eat a burger and fries at a highway diner because that's your only option, you'll naturally bring your thoughts, emotions, and actions back in alignment with your intent and take more healthy action.

Each day you'll be manifesting your dream, gently correcting yourself when you start thinking, *But I'm not losing weight fast enough* or *I hate exercising.* These are concerns that occur at the level of jaguar, where you write stories that turn into disappointments. When you dream, you'll probably continue to experience judgmental thoughts such as these, but you'll quickly correct them.

Finally, with eagle consciousness, you'll be able to hold on to the big picture of cultivating health and respecting your body. You'll find the creativity to overcome all those obstacles you perceive at jaguar. You'll remember that you're on a hummingbird-like journey that twists and turns, and that none of us is in perfect alignment with our intent every second of our lives.

Reject Perfection

When we're caught up in our mental stories, we look to heroes as examples of perfection and become disappointed if we learn that they are human, like us. We want these people to be symbols of flawlessness, idealized demigods rather than human beings. When we ignore their flaws, we have a convenient excuse to let ourselves off the hook for our own behaviors because we can tell ourselves that we can't possibly live up to the standards of our larger-than-life heroes. We'll say things like, "Ah, what am I, Mother Teresa? Christ on the cross?" and justify our less-than-compassionate acts by declaring, "Hey, I'm no saint."

We don't want to hear that Martin Luther King, Jr., had extramarital affairs, or that John Lennon wrote that all we need is love but barely had a relationship with his oldest son. After all, these are reminders that even flawed human beings are capable of great deeds, which will then cause that nagging little voice inside ourselves to ask, "So why are *you* not engaging in great deeds?"

Rather than projecting all our positive qualities onto celebrities, we can choose to embrace our own ability to be intrepid and original. Our heroes' flaws don't erase their courageous acts, and if we acknowledge our own failings, we'll find that our weaknesses won't overwhelm us, paralyze us, or keep us from courageous action.

All of us can do great things even if we tend to be impatient, arrogant, irritable, or anxious. Even the Dalai Lama can't possibly be perfectly compassionate at all times. Maybe he doesn't grouse about the airline-reservation specialist accidentally screwing up his itinerary as most of us would, but I like to believe that he does have his judgmental and angry moments. And we know that Jesus himself kicked over a few tables and threw a first-class tantrum one day when his irritation and frustration got the better of him.

We don't need any more mythological heroes. There's nothing more paralyzing than the notion of perfection—we feel that we can never attain it, so why bother to even try? No, what we need is to be honest about what it means to be human: that we are fated to miss the mark of perfection but achieve small and impressive acts of courage and greatness.

Instead of thinking that some people are flawless, we ought to take inspiration from the fact that our heroes, celebrated or not, brought themselves back on course again and again whenever they realized that their behavior was out of alignment with their intent. Simply saying, "Enough—I'm moving on!" is an act of courage that breaks the spell.

If you aim to be perfect, you'll feel disheartened and slip back into the nightmare. Instead of dreaming courageously, you'll feel victimized by a lack of opportunities, your sluggish metabolism, your low salary, your tendency toward depression, or some other apparent obstacle to your forward movement. There will be no end to the reasons why you can't live up to your ideals, and you'll forget that you are in charge of the dream. Let go of your reasons for not achieving the life you want and find rightness in your life in this moment, whatever your circumstances, whatever your failings. Release your need to be perfect and above reproach. It's not going to happen.

You can improve your mood and feel a sense of power and control over your existence by ending each day thinking about three things that happened to you that you're grateful for and identifying what role you played in manifesting these three situations. When you find yourself feeling that your life isn't what it should be, dwelling on what isn't working, or berating yourself for what you haven't accomplished, try this simple act of recognizing your power to courageously dream, as well as how you've affected your world and the people around you today.

Reject Grandiosity

In a culture that overvalues individuality, we're taught that we should try to stand out from the crowd, to be unique and different. To do so means that we have to compete with everyone around us to be number one, which is not easy to manage. Caught up in the stressful game of competition, we start to desire grandiosity, thunderous applause, and validation of our tremendous importance in the world. Remember, the need for grandiosity is rooted in our illusion that we can create security by acquiring approval from others. This illusion is at the heart of the lust for fame that so many of us in the West suffer from: We're convinced that we were born with a special mission that someday we and others will recognize.

Many of my clients' main concern is: "What should I do with the rest of my life?" They wonder what their special calling is, what their guiding mission should be for their remaining years. I hesitate to respond with the obvious answer, which is: "Nothing." I gently point out that until they let go of the need to be special, they can't create their calling and learn to chart their way through life with courage and creativity. Until then, they'll continue to look outside themselves for a "call" that only comes from within.

Courage helps us let go of the need to be "the best of the best" and instead allows us to focus on being the best that we can be. When we're courageous, we stop caring about whether our neighbors are talking about how wonderful we are, and our zeal for being the crusader or messiah dissipates. We simply find the moral courage to live according to our principles, the intellectual courage to explore new ideas, and the emotional courage to be honest with ourselves and others. We don't feel the need to be surrounded by adoring fans—with eagle courage, we're true to ourselves, living our destiny wholeheartedly. Our neediness, and the sense of lack that drives our grandiosity, starts to go away.

We all know people who live small lives yet feel that they can influence the fate of nations, right now, in their lifetime. I have a friend, for instance, who's convinced that he has the formula for ending hunger in Africa, if people would only listen to him. And every cab driver in Manhattan will tell you what's wrong with the city and how *they* would fix it.

Such individuals can be so earnest and self-righteous that it's exasperating. Caught up in the grandiose nightmare of being noble rescuers, they blind themselves to the power they have to change the world in humble, quiet ways. They ignore others' small acts of bravery; more than that, they insist that anyone who focuses on such acts is deluding themselves and wasting time. They become petulant when the world doesn't conform to their demands and then put their heads down and try to calculate exactly how to build their power base, obsessing over their strategies.

In contrast, the men and women who actually do have the power to influence nations are usually focused on ideas that play out in small and often unexpected ways. They're uninterested in changing the world single-handedly, and they're unassuming and quick to laugh at themselves because the appearance of power and prestige doesn't matter very much to them.

For example, when Thomas Jefferson was President of the United States, his staff members wrung their hands over his penchant for greeting visitors to the White House in his slippers and robe, with his scraggly red hair free from his formal white wig. He claimed he was just too busy to attend to such fussy details. Similarly, Benjamin Franklin was a great statesman, and a very important figure in the creation of our nation, but he readily joked about his appetite for wine and his eye for the ladies.

Neither man took himself too seriously, but each believed passionately in his vision of a new type of country and took responsibility for creating and cultivating the new democracy. What Jefferson and Franklin didn't do is try to micromanage the details or shut out dissenting voices. They exposed themselves to different ideas, listened to others, and were willing to admit they didn't always know everything—and indeed, they didn't. Both had significant personal flaws: Jefferson was personally opposed to slavery but was a slave owner himself, had a long sexual relationship with one of his slaves, and allowed his own biracial children to be enslaved for several years. Benjamin Franklin had a very troubled relationship with his son, who disappointed Franklin and didn't live up to his standards. Yet despite their weaknesses, neither Jefferson nor Franklin hid behind their prestigious reputations or pretended to be anything other than human.

Grandiose people with a desire for reform become the petty tyrants of the world, so infatuated with their own self-image that they ignore other opinions and risk the fate of many to support their illusion of "the Great Rescuer." Each of us needs to be cautious about our potential for becoming a dictator in our own life and guard against insisting that the world has to listen to and obey us for its own good. It's far more rewarding to be the person who quietly puts in unpaid overtime to do a good deed for an individual who's struggling or suffering—and who also stands up to the CEO at the next staff meeting to say, "Since you attribute our record corporate profits to our outstanding customer service, how much of a raise will we employees be getting?"

One of the most effective ways to prevent grandiosity is to be attuned to the symbols of our dreams, which tip us off to what our conscious mind resists recognizing.

Recognize and Decode the Symbols of Your Dreams

The dreams that unfold in your sleep are full of symbols created by your subconscious, and to understand their message, you have to decode them. Psychologists tell us that water often represents emotion, basements of buildings stand in for the subconscious, and images can be visual puns—so being confused by the route of the #15 bus in your dream might symbolize being puzzled over your 15-year-old's behavior.

If you're not conscious of something in your life that you need to attend to, you'll probably experience dreams with recurring themes. You may keep finding yourself in the same boutique where every item of designer clothing is on sale but nothing fits you; or perhaps you notice that you're continually running from something, such as a monster, a crazy person, or an angry dog. Your subconscious will create these symbols in your nighttime reverie in order to awaken you. Ignore them, and they won't go away.

Whereas in the West we're interested in what a certain symbol means, I'm more interested in the moods, feelings, and awareness that a particular symbol or image evokes. We usually take a symbol from the soul and interpret it at the jaguar level of the mind, where water and basements mean something in particular. This can be extremely valuable because we can get clear directives from our subconscious that can be very helpful in our lives. Yet it's just as important to keep dreams at the level of hummingbird, without immediately analyzing what they mean, and simply look for that dreamtime symbol or theme in our waking lives. The significance of the symbol is then provided by nature and the chance occurrence of events that Carl Jung called synchronicity, rather than by the analytic mind.

So, for example, if I dreamed about provisioning a ship to set out on a journey with two friends, I'd look for these symbols over the following days: a journey or new beginning; two allies; nurturing (provisioning) myself; or the start of a new project. If any of these symbols showed up around me, I'd connect them in my mind with my dream. This cuts across the barrier between waking and sleeping dreams, and it frees the torrent of unconscious energy in my psyche and makes these resources available to me during my waking state.

When you're awake, your life is filled with symbols, and they'll come into your life again and again, mirroring a message from your subconscious. These daytime signs can alert you to opportunities as well as to a tendency toward wanting to be the noble rescuer, believing that you're justified in being a bully, or feeling sorry for yourself. By returning often to hummingbird perception, you'll not only notice the powerful symbols in your day- and nighttime dreams, you'll start to understand them much more easily, without having to overthink them. So when you're being chased in a dream, instead of only trying to figure out who or what is chasing you in real life, you'll choose not to perceive yourself as a victim of circumstances. Then whatever is chasing you will stop giving pursuit, both in your dreamtime and your waking life.

Recently, I dreamed that I was in a building where a wall had collapsed, and I was going through the rubble with my young daughter. We reached a table and found that there was a cash register on it. The drawer was open, and I knew that the money in it belonged to us. We started taking the bills, and I told my daughter to grab the rolls of coins, too, because we had to rebuild this house in another location.

On the surface, from a jaguar perspective, the theme of this dream might appear to be "Take the money and run before it all collapses around you." However, as I looked more carefully into it, I realized that I had a choice of multiple interpretations. An obvious one was to consider taking it literally, from the level of serpent, and cashing in and building a cabin in the woods somewhere. Yet I chose another interpretation, from the level of hummingbird—one I decided to heed—which was to construct a new home for the body of knowledge that every Earthkeeper is entrusted with, since the walls of the indigenous house that protected this wisdom were collapsing.

There are very few shamanic societies left that haven't been contaminated by Western consumerism. Even in the most remote regions of the Amazon, the inhabitants recognize a Coca-Cola logo. So this dream was telling me that I'd have all the support, both financial and familial, that I needed to help build a new spiritual home for the wisdom of the Earthkeepers. While my daughter symbolized that I'd be doing this for future generations, I was also being cautioned that I needed to be careful not to get caught in a grandiose vision where I'd be the noble rescuer of an indigenous shamanic tradition. Otherwise, the building itself could collapse on me.

Let's now turn to decoding your own dreams' messages.

The Symbols of Your Waking Dreams

Finding the symbols in our waking life that are most powerful to us at any given time is as easy as remembering our early-morning dreams. Many symbols are shared collectively by all of humanity, but others derive from our culture and our personal experiences. We all know the meaning of certain symbolic acts, such as when someone burns an American flag at a demonstration or puts on a Richard Nixon mask, but in our own lives, we'll often have strong feelings about symbols that represent stories we've created.

When you discover a symbol in your waking dream, you can use emotional courage to set aside your discomfort and explore what it means. Intellectual courage will allow you to think in a new way and discard any old, disempowering beliefs; while courage of the soul will let you create the dream you truly desire. Become aware of these symbols and get into the habit of deciphering them, noticing the context and situations that they reappear in, and you may well awaken to truths you've overlooked.

What does a certain celebrity you judgmentally gossip about represent for you—your own unrequited dreams, perhaps, or your resentment that you don't have unlimited funds, time, and freedom to fritter away? What does the number 200 on the bathroom scale mean to you? What does that dent on your car point to? By examining your strong responses to symbols in your waking life, you can recognize whether you've gotten trapped in a nightmare and forgotten how to dream courageously.

You can now write a more empowering story than one of a "fat and undesirable person," a "financial failure," or an "underappreciated person who doesn't have 'enough' to live a happy life"; and then you'll stop gritting your teeth whenever someone asks, "So, are you still single?" With the courage to dream, you can say no to the old ideas about what ought to make you happy or miserable and create something more empowering.

Symbols of Grandiosity

Mother Teresa said that there are no great acts, only small acts performed with great love. Yet too often, rather than following her words and actions, we aspire to *be* the next Mother Teresa—albeit without all the sacrifices. Instead of desiring to make a difference in the world in whatever way we can and opening our eyes to all the opportunities for doing so, we'll proclaim, "I want to make a billion dollars so I can rescue the world!" After all, a billion dollars symbolizes great power.

We become convinced that to live a meaningful life, it's not enough to parent one child well or touch the lives of a few people who are spending their last days in a hospice where we volunteer; we want the *USA Today* article lauding us for personally curing all the sorrow in the world through our hard work, dedication, and genius. And if someone else's book ends up on the *New York Times* bestseller list, or even if they have a daughter who's elected prom queen, we're envious because they've achieved the symbols of power and importance we crave.

Whenever you find yourself creating grandiose goals and getting fixated on symbols of success, it's a sign that you're stuck in jaguar, looking to achieve the false security of fame, power, and social approval. People who actually do dream a better world into being experience great joy in the small acts. They're the ones who are happy to serve the world in their own small and quiet way; and they don't become overwhelmed by the amount of work needed to end poverty, violence, and destruction of the planet. They're the village priests in South America who labor to help their flock of indigenous people despite pressure from Rome to conform to the Catholic Church's priorities, or the local grandmother who tirelessly works to encourage her neighbors to replace the herbicides on their lawns with natural weedkillers.

When you're dreaming at the level of soul, you spot your opportunities and find the courage to act rather than giving up in despair. Nor do you become cynical, shrugging your shoulders and saying, "I can't participate—I'm far too busy," "Ah, it's no big deal," and "Someone else will take care of the problem, I'm sure." What's more, when you dream courageously, the resources you need to make a difference in the world will show up, whether what you require is a billion dollars, creative ideas, dreaming partners, or the guts to stand up against the status quo.

If your focus is on acquiring that billion dollars so that you can finally begin living a happy, fulfilled life, then what you wish for is a daydream that can't manifest in the present. You lock yourself out of achieving it because the goal is conditional. A dream is always unconditional. Dream, and you accept whatever the conditions are. You make a difference in the world every day, regardless of your situation or what resources are at hand.

Unlike goals, which have an end point, dreams are a way of life. Visions of the soul have passion fueling them, which is why they find ways to manifest in the world without the use of force or willpower. Some of my clients are very wealthy, and I've found that the ones who are extremely successful in business aren't in it for the money but for the chance to express their passion and creativity, and it's that passion that results in their generating money. They're living lives of abundance—abundant ideas, abundant feelings of gratitude and joy, and abundant feelings of curiosity and wonder.

In the following exercise, you'll begin to awaken to the symbols of grandiosity you've clung to and find the courage to discard them.

Exercise: Giving Up Your Symbols of Grandiosity

Ask yourself, "What do I feel I need to have to signal how very important I am?" Is it an expensive car? A job title that makes people look at you in awe? A Rolex watch? A trophy wife, wealthy husband, or child who attends an Ivy League school? The latest information on a controversial topic? The most salacious piece of gossip? A caustic attitude that intimidates others? A terrible childhood trauma that left you with no self-esteem? Remember that your symbol of grandiosity might be an object, a label, or a behavior that you believe communicates the message that you're someone special who's deserving of respect, pity, or awe.

Try becoming like a monk and giving up your symbol of grandiosity for a time just to see what it feels like. If you measure your importance by how attractive and smart you are, dress down and attend a gathering of people where you do your best to ask questions but don't provide information unless asked. Stop yourself from the need to be sarcastic or one-up others with references to your job title, who you know, or what trendy neighborhood you live in. If you feel that you're very important because you engage in a great deal of community service, volunteer to do the least glamorous job for a while and let others take the more prestigious positions. If you actually feel insignificant and unimportant, try telling the group about a great deed you've attempted.

Pay attention to your discomfort, not judging it but simply noticing it. Ask yourself, "Where is this coming from?" Let the answer arise, and allow yourself to be amused by your attachment to grandiosity. Now set your intent to release your fears of disapproval.

Cultivate Mindfulness

To spot our everyday opportunities for courage, we need to cultivate *mindfulness,* which simply means paying attention to what's happening right now. Mindfulness means that we don't get lost in thoughts about what might happen tomorrow or what *did* happen yesterday; instead, we give our undivided attention to whatever we're doing right now.

It can be difficult to practice mindfulness in our culture, which encourages us to stay overstimulated and rush about rather than slow down and become calm, aware, and contemplative. Yet people who are aware and fully present in the moment experience grace. Honest about their true needs and rejecting fear, they have no need to buy lots of stuff to alleviate any feelings of insecurity or to goose the economy. Mindful people are not easily manipulated or scared into following the plans of egotistical leaders, which makes it hard for power-hungry and grandiose bullies to intimidate them. I find it amusing that the word *conspiracy* comes from the Latin *conspirare,* which means "to breathe together." Tyrants have always been frightened of people who practice mindfulness. Such individuals break the rules and upset the status quo; by being mindful, they access their hummingbird wisdom and dream courageously.

Mindfulness is a habit that's easier to develop when you make a point of doing something daily that trains your jaguar mind to stop wandering off in every direction and sniffing behind every tree. Regular meditation is a great way to develop mindfulness. Try sitting on a cushion and slowing down your breathing so that you can begin to distance yourself from your rushing stream of thoughts. As you observe your breath, watch those thoughts float in front of you like ever-changing clouds, and you'll experience that they aren't so important after all.

Mindful awareness requires being fully present in your body, on the cushion, in the room, right at the present moment. This awareness carries over into everyday life, and you'll find it easier to recognize when you've started sleepwalking. You'll find that when you're caught up in a story, a part of you will say, "Huh, look at me, playing the victim here," and you'll be reminded of your intent to live courageously. In that moment, you'll discover that you can easily drop the old yarn instead of embellishing it. This awareness quickly pops you out of your jaguar consciousness into the dreaming realm of hummingbird.

If you don't feel comfortable engaging in traditional meditation practice, there are other ways to cultivate mindfulness. You can simply sit quietly at your desk for a few minutes, for instance, and breathe while you observe your mind. You can engage in physical exercise that slows down your rapid stream of thoughts and causes you to breathe more deeply so that you have more clarity of mind.

Or you can regularly journal to train your mind to remain in the present moment.

If you find yourself resisting any form of practice that slows you down and causes you to become more aware, it may be because your mind is struggling to repress a subconscious thought or memory that it knows will cause you pain once you experience it. An organizational expert I know says she finds that her clients who keep themselves continually busy and on the run are often creating this rushed, manic mind-set in order to avoid some incredibly painful thought, such as a memory of abuse they've repressed.

Allow yourself to stop running—become aware of what you've been avoiding so that you can address it.

Install Intent in Your Soul

The more mindful you become, and the more you start to understand the symbols in your life, the more you'll recognize when your actions are out of sync with your intent. When your behavior contradicts your dream, it may be because it's merely an idea or wish created in your mind, not a true intent that you're experiencing at the soul level. Or you may become distracted and get stuck in lower levels of consciousness, forgetting all that you recognize whenever you're in hummingbird or eagle awareness.

Rituals can help you install your intent at the level of the soul if you perform them with the genuine desire to shift your level of consciousness. If you allow yourself to remain stuck in jaguar awareness, you'll fuss about where to stand, what to say, and what to do; and you'll expect the ceremony to shift your feelings and perception without your having to open up to its power. This is the case whether you're at a Catholic Mass, a bar mitzvah, a shamanic ceremony—or simply lighting a candle before you share a dinner with your beloved. Performed properly, rituals create an open space that allows you to access a higher state of awareness. When the emphasis is on the details of how the ritual should be performed and the desired outcome, it becomes an empty ceremony.

So if you rush to get everyone to the holiday table at a particular time and gobble down the meal before the ball game starts, it should be no surprise that once again, your annual family get-together left everyone feeling unmoved and disconnected. When you go to your yoga class with a competitive attitude, proud that you can hold a pose longer than anyone else can, you won't shift into a deeper awareness of the body and a more fluid movement of physical energy; you'll probably just pull a muscle and leave class feeling defeated.

But if you surrender to the moment, remaining open to the creativity of the universe working through you and the people around you, the actions of the ritual will help you shift your consciousness and install your intent at the level of soul. Whether you're performing a personal ritual or participating with others, commit yourself to being open and spontaneous.

I'm reminded of a couple I know, who asked a friend of theirs who's an amateur singer to participate in their wedding ceremony by leading everyone in a popular song about supporting those you love. The singer was nervous and started off-key, but soon a few others joined in and he fell into the right key, singing confidently and with great feeling. By the end of the song, everyone present had been so moved by the coming together of voices to support one another—and the newly married couple—that they burst into applause. Sometimes the best part of the ritual is when someone makes a "mistake" because it wakes everyone up to the meaning and shakes off any complacency that causes them to merely go through the motions of a ceremony.

To install intent in your soul, you must awaken to the creativity that's available to you at the level of hummingbird consciousness, where ritual, poetry, and metaphor arise as if magically expressing what's in your heart. The following exercise can help you reclaim your creativity and allow you to tap into that consciousness.

Exercise: Haiku of Life

A haiku is a form of poetry that generally consists of three lines in which the first and last contain five syllables, while the middle is made up of seven. The subject is usually the natural world, a topic that tends to awaken people to their sense of oneness with the divine. Following are a couple examples of this type of poem.

The first one is a haiku I composed myself:

Peach blossoms in spring
fresh deer tracks grace my morning
new life arising.

Next is one by the Japanese poet Bufu:

Oh, I don't care
where autumn clouds
are drifting to.

Finally, this was written by the poet Chine:

It lights up
as lightly as it fades
a firefly.

Try your hand at writing some haikus about nature. Don't do this at home in your air-conditioned apartment while staring at your orchid desktop picture—actually get out in nature. Once seated in your backyard or on a park bench, empty your mind of thoughts about your to-do list or the dreadful state of the world, your job, or your health at the moment. Observe the trees, the grass, the birds, and the insects; and then write a few poems. Let go of any judgments such as *I can't do this* or *I have no talent for writing.* Just do it.

When you've finished writing your haikus, read them over several times, allowing yourself to feel the poetry you've expressed, and release any judgmental thoughts.

Next, compose three haikus about an aspect of your life that you feel absolutely no sense of creativity about or that you find it very difficult to express any courage for. Write three poems about your tense relationship with your father or your teenage daughter, or dedicate them to your airless cubicle at work. Wax poetic about your poor eating habits or that pack of cigarettes that you've secretly hidden underneath the seat of your car.

The point is to discover the beauty, humor, and poetry in your ugliness and self-loathing. This is the first step in accessing your courage: accepting what is, without judgment. Once you've taken this step, you can take the next one, rewriting a new story called "My Journey out of the Dark Underworld of Fear and Conformity."

≈≈≈

Indulge in creativity whenever you can. You don't necessarily have to produce a work of art such as a poem, song, or painting; but if you strive to live with originality and openness to possibility, you'll be inspired to dream.

Each of us can be a true iconoclast who looks at what everyone else is seeing and perceives it just a little bit differently. Children do this quite naturally: What they see in a work of abstract art, or even an everyday event, is often surprising because their take is so fresh and original.

The Earthkeepers recognize that to live courageously, dreaming a better world in each moment and opening ourselves to true originality, we must engage in three core disciplines. These practices help us reject self-judgment, connect with our intent, and easily and naturally act with courage. The three core disciplines, which I've devoted the next three chapters of this book to, are: (1) practice truth; (2) clean up your river; and (3) be ready to die at any instant.

∼∼∼∼∼

CHAPTER SEVEN

Practice Truth

*You can only find truth if you seek it
for yourself, for the truths of history are
the truths of others. But truth is like a mirage
in the desert. For us, the task is not to chase truth
but to create it. Truth is a stance, an act
of power that you bring to all your actions.
Truth is what the person of knowledge
brings to every moment.*
— *from Dance of the Four Winds*
BY ALBERTO VILLOLDO (written with Erik Jendresen)

The discipline we're going to focus on in the next several pages is one of the great teachings of the Earthkeepers. It states that when we practice truth, everything we speak becomes true: Whatever we say comes to pass because our word is golden. When we don't practice it, everything we say and do becomes a lie.

The practice of truth requires vigilance, honesty, and acceptance of ourselves and others. It begins with mindfulness, as well as not pretending that little acts of cowardice are unimportant. When we're not mindful, we're sleepwalking; when we are, we notice that something isn't sitting right with us, which opens us up to ask truth-eliciting questions such as "Why am I so uncomfortable?" "What thought is making me unhappy?" and "What unsettling feeling am I experiencing?" There are also a few core practices within the discipline of truth, including those of nonjudgment and transparency, that helps us understand how little control we actually have of our lives—that Spirit is always in charge.

Whenever you're hiding from an uncomfortable truth, life will draw your attention to it by providing you with situations that challenge you to stop the charade. If you choose to ignore these signals, your body may very well give you a wake-up call. A story created when you avoided a painful realization will become buried in your subconscious and imprinted in your LEF. Eventually, it will manifest its energies as a physical ailment.

We can avoid this fate if we consciously choose to rewrite the stories we've created. Every illness we suffer is a potential reminder to edit our tales and rise to a higher level of consciousness. Then we discover that there's a spiritual solution to every problem we face, since at the level of eagle and Spirit, all ailments turn into opportunities for learning.

If you're scared or angry, you'll find that you can experience these emotions in a very physical way. Your heart rate and muscle tension will increase, your breathing will become shallow, your palms might become sweaty, and you may even tremble with rage or fear. Such physiological experiences are part of the primitive, instinctual, fight-or-flight response, which is meant to give you the energy to battle a dangerous foe or flee a situation before you're harmed.

In the modern world, however, the jaguar mind has convinced us that any threat we perceive is highly dangerous. Ancient people experienced the urge to defend themselves or run away when a cave bear came barreling toward them; we experience it when someone tells us we're irresponsible and incompetent, or when the person we're dating says, "I think we should see other people." Practicing truth rarely requires us to face down a cave bear, but it can certainly feel that way.

If someone looks at you a little too long and you're sure that he or she is disapproving of you, it can be difficult to refrain from acting out old stories—after all, you feel like you're under attack and really want to lash out at this individual. But you can learn to pay attention to your body's response to the perceived threat and choose to change your thoughts, feelings, and behaviors.

When your fight-or-flight response becomes locked in the *on* position, you live in fear and perceive everything with the eyes of jaguar. Your terror keeps you from practicing truth, which requires a discipline of fearlessness and the development of eagle consciousness. However, the regular exercise of certain habits—such as slow breathing, walking out of a room during a heated argument in order to regroup, or consciously creating reflective thoughts such as *I wonder why I'm feeling threatened right now*—can help dial down the need to attack or run, thus pulling you out of reactive jaguar consciousness.

In the Amazon, they refer to this practice as "bringing the jaguar down from the tree," because when our jaguar mind has been frightened, it behaves like a cat perched on high branches, hissing at anyone who comes near. While the shamans have energetic practices for resetting the fight-or-flight response back to the neutral position, we can accomplish the same thing through the practice of mindfulness.

Embrace Nonjudgment and Transparency

Once we're vigilant about how we're acting in a given situation, we can let go of the stories that lock us into judgments such as *I must be unlovable if I can behave so badly* or *She's not a good person if she could act that way toward me.* We recognize that there are certainly ugly situations that cause people pain, but we can just conclude that they're awful without rushing to judge the victims, rescuers, and bullies.

Practicing nonjudgment allows us to see the larger picture, including the bully's fear, which is driving her aggressive, offensive behavior; the victim's lack of courage, along with his complicity in maintaining the situation; and the rescuer's focus on himself and his need to be the righteous hero. Practicing truth means slowing down, stepping back, and looking at a situation from all angles to get a better understanding of all that's happening without having the view clouded by personal assumptions.

In Judaism (and early Christianity), there's a sin known as *loshon hora,* which refers to engaging in gossip. According to loshon hora, speaking negatively about someone for no constructive purpose is equivalent to cursing them, and listening in on gossip is as bad as spreading it yourself because you're actively participating in it. But according to Jewish law, you must tell the truth about someone, even if it happens to be ugly or painful, to prevent an innocent person from being harmed. In that case, it's important to speak the facts only, without judgment, as that can only be dispensed by God. If you aren't going to prevent another person from being harmed, it's best to remain silent and not speak poorly about anyone, regardless of how great the temptation is.

Once you see the larger picture and remember that everyone has his or her own journey of spiritual maturation, it's easier to let go of the need to judge everyone and everything. Then you can practice truth and be who you really are: true to your values and operating with integrity and courage.

Similarly, the practice of transparency means allowing yourself to be seen by others for who you are, having nothing to hide. To that end, not long ago I was watching a news program in which a political pundit was being confronted by a caller who was pleading with her to tone down her notoriously caustic remarks about a political foe. While the expert interrupted the caller with sarcastic comments, she hid behind large sunglasses, flipped her hair constantly, and aggressively tried to change the subject. For all her attempts to appear nonchalant, her body language and efforts to deflect the criticism left no doubt that she was feeling insecure and exposed.

It's curious, but the more we try to hide our flaws and insecurity, the more visible they are to others. We like to believe that we can put on a good enough act to fool everyone, including ourselves, but we fail miserably and suffer even more as we continue to deceive ourselves.

With courage, you can practice transparency. You can give up your attempts to look powerful, influential, humble, or wise—you can simply be who you are, with no veneers hiding the real you from the rest of the world. Part the curtains, let reality shine through, and be as unashamed of your failings and weaknesses as you are of your strength and power. You don't have to fear letting people see your humanity because like everyone else, you can't help acting foolish, greedy, selfish, insensitive, or scared at times. But becoming transparent also means allowing your beauty and courage to shine and be seen by others. If you practice this, you'll no longer need to scurry about, trying to protect your reputation or create status and security in the material world. You'll accept yourself right now, in this moment, and let your own beauty shine, allowing your elegance and grace to inspire others to find their beauty.

The moment you stop hiding from yourself is the moment you step into the flow of creativity—where you can choose to think, act, and feel differently—and you can be reborn and redeemed in that very instant. You don't need to keep whipping yourself, hoping for redemption from some god on high, for the second you no longer conceal anything from yourself you clear your toxic thoughts, feelings, and behaviors. That's not to say you don't have to make amends; it just means that you begin the process of redemption and rebirth the moment you allow yourself to be seen, regardless of what your story is. Your actions are already in the past, so you can move on and change the way you're operating right now. Then you'll find the courage and impetus to clean up any damage you've done.

Practicing transparency requires that you draw on your highest levels of courage and dream from the level of the soul. But if you're to practice truth, you must recognize—and accept—that everything you've created around you is a mirage.

Reject the Illusion of Safety and Control

All that we experience around us and have made for ourselves—our power and status, our belief that we're living daringly and creatively, and our sense of safety—are lies. We've created it all so that we can feel in control of the nightmare. Our entire existence, in fact, is a story based on our need to produce and foster the myth that we're safe and in control of our lives at all times.

We want to believe that we have security in this world and are the masters of our fate, but that's simply not the case. Every one of us is part of the flowing river of life, carried along wherever Spirit chooses to take us. We work with Spirit to move the waters this way or that, and we're in charge of how we perceive ourselves and our world, but Spirit's will is holding the reins when it comes to the facts of our lives. We buy into our illusion of control in order to quell the fears we experience at serpent and jaguar, but we're never fooled for long. The universe provides plenty of reminders that none of us is truly in charge, no matter what we do. For example, I choose to eat healthy foods, exercise daily, and meditate; but I recognize that even if I take all sorts of precautions, I still don't have the power to ensure that I'll never experience any health problems. Even those of us who could be called "health nuts" can end up with cancer, heart disease, multiple sclerosis, and other ailments . . . and, of course, accidents happen, too. (The same is true for opportunity, which knocks on our door at the oddest times.)

At the same time, we must understand that it's not functional to let fears about what might happen prevent us from making good decisions about our health and safety in the physical world. We can't let the fact that we have a finite number of days left on this earth overwhelm and paralyze us; after all, if we do, we'll be so terrified that we'll refuse to walk outside or take any risks whatsoever.

To live daringly and creatively, to courageously dream, doesn't require us to give up sensible habits or our health insurance. It does require that we be aware that in life, there are always matters that are out of our control. There's no relationship insurance, for instance, and the truth is that love sometimes ends, but we need to be open to it anyway. Likewise, there's no shame insurance, but we still need to speak our truth regardless of whether someone might ridicule us. If we tell ourselves that we can micromanage our lives and avoid all sorrow or misfortune, we'll get stuck in lower levels of consciousness, desperately trying to build a fortress against disaster.

Practicing truth means being willing to consider that everything we say and do is a lie designed to perpetuate the nest we've built for ourselves in the physical world: our social reputation, our marriage, our career, our house, our credit rating, and so on. The more strongly we hold on to our illusion of safety and control, the harder it is to access the creative well that's available to us. Once we let go of the notion that we're in control of our lives, we begin to understand that the hand of Spirit has always been guiding us, but we've simply been unaware of this fact. Then we can turn the wheel over to the One who has always been in charge. This doesn't mean that we no longer need to steer our ship and trim sail, but rather that we don't have to fight the winds. Ultimately, like Jonah, we accept that Spirit may want us in Nineveh, and we respond to our calling there.

So often we tell ourselves lies about who we are so that we'll feel secure in our identity, thus not having to do the hard work of facing our failings. When we believe our own press releases, we're like the smoker who claims that she doesn't really light up, except for that post-dinner cigarette each day . . . and, well, the one before bed . . . and the pack she reaches for when she's really under stress, which isn't all the time, so you can't really count those. . . . We're like the fellow driving the car with the bumper sticker PRACTICE RANDOM ACTS OF KINDNESS who cuts someone else off to get into the parking space first.

Accept who you are, laugh about your foibles, and allow others to see the real you rather than presenting them with a smoke-and-mirrors act designed to trick them into believing that you're someone you're not. Don't follow the example of an acquaintance of mine, who's very wealthy and insists on telling everyone he meets, from waiters to cab drivers, who he is and whom he knows. He isn't comfortable when he's not in his story, so he hides his true self.

Then there's another friend of mine, an exotic and beautiful single woman who doesn't believe in fear or dishonesty. When she's asked what she does for a living, she'll reply with a straight face, "I'm in the hospitality industry . . . I'm cleaning houses right now." It's great fun to watch the looks on people's faces and to see men make feeble excuses for moving away from her at a party after she's made this revelation. Apparently, they don't want to date someone who's "just a maid."

When you practice truth, you're unconcerned about appearances and aren't afraid of being exposed. You recognize that "rich man" and "housekeeper" are just stories that aren't terribly useful ones for describing who you are today, since you're so much more than what you do or have accomplished.

The moment you have the courage to look into the mirror and observe your reflection in all its beauty and ugliness is the moment in which that reflection begins to change.

Practice Truth Through Intellectual Courage

You can't practice truth without having the intellectual courage to admit that you don't know it all. A simple act of this type of courage might be admitting to a group of people that you haven't made up your mind on some political issue because you're still trying to learn more about the subject, and then not feeling embarrassed or ashamed if they look down on you because of your admission. In fact, ultimately you must be brave enough to admit to *yourself* that you don't know anything other than a collection of facts. Truth then ceases to be a quest to find people who have the same spin on reality that you do, those individuals whom you can readily agree with. Instead truth becomes a stance, a gesture that you bring to every moment and every engagement. You no longer seek truth, but you do bring it to every situation, no matter how uncomfortable it might be to do so.

We live in a world where we're constantly exposed to spin doctors who tell us what we should think before we've had a moment to process the raw information. The media knows that we lack intellectual courage and want the false security of having a solid, defensible opinion right away. I once turned on a 24-hour-news channel, for instance, and only saw an empty podium where a politician was about to show up and speak. Over this image an expert eagerly pondered what could happen if the speaker said this as opposed to that, as well as what may occur next week if someone else were to respond by saying such and such. The speculation grew increasingly absurd while the camera betrayed the gap between the reality of nothing going on and the illusion that if we could just get enough of a handle on what might possibly take place in the future, we'd all feel better.

It's unfortunate that so many individuals try to put others down by pulling out some obscure factoid that seemingly proves the superiority of their position. It's tempting to fall into this type of dishonest discourse in our own lives: We're quick to tell ourselves that we know the whole picture when we're usually missing some vital information or an important perspective. At our jobs and in our relationships, we never want to admit that we lack certain skills or need to polish others. Instead, we create excuses and become hostile and sarcastic so that the men and women in our lives are too intimidated to confront us.

We use jargon so that we'll sound smarter than we are. We'll even team up with other people who are missing skills and feeling insecure just like we are, thus forming a united front against the one person who exhibits the intellectual courage to say, "Hey, you guys, I think we're screwing up here." This is exactly how we ended up with the military ordering $600 toilet seats or hospitals charging $12 for Band-Aids and ibuprofen. Practicing truth means being the first one to acknowledge that some new thinking needs to happen, to admit that "I need to find out some more information or develop some skills before I can make a good decision."

Practice Truth Through Emotional and Moral Courage

Emotional and moral courage allows us to be honest about our real feelings and take responsibility for our actions in all of our relationships; it demands that we love truthfully and vulnerably. When we don't practice this kind of courage, we become unrepentant hypocrites in denial of our dishonesty. And we become this way because admitting to the gap between our intentions and our behaviors can make us extremely uncomfortable.

Here's an example from my own life. I used to live in a well-to-do suburb in the Southeast, where I met a couple who had lived in the area for generations. While their parents and grandparents had never accepted anyone who wasn't Caucasian, Christian, or Southern into their social world, this new generation had decided to be courageous, break the old rules, and reach out to individuals whom their forebears would have rejected outright. However, they didn't actually want to dream into being a new, more inclusive country club and neighborhood—they just liked the sound of it.

My wife and I got an invitation to dine at the club; during dinner, our new friends smiled broadly as they told us that there was normally a five-year wait to become members, along with a $60,000 initiation fee, but they were willing to waive both if we'd join. Naturally I asked them why they were making such a generous offer, and they said it was because although my wife was Jewish and I was Cuban, we were both light-skinned. This meant that we could help them show others that this country club was open to ethnic people without upsetting the other members too much by inviting, say, an African-American couple to join.

My wife and I were completely stunned by this revelation. Clearly, our neighbors thought that their compromise was quite clever; however, the way we saw it, they were being hypocrites. Not being the country-club type anyway, I decided to see just how comfortable they'd be with me as a fellow member and proceeded to tell them about working with shamans in the Amazon. Apparently, our so-called friends decided that my wife and I were just a bit *too* colorful to be a part of their social circle, and we were never offered an invitation to join them again.

When we practice truth, we're not dipping a toe into the river—we're jumping into its rushing waters and getting ourselves sopping wet. There can be no timidity, no compromise, no halfway measures; if we try to practice truth just a little bit, we end up becoming hypocrites.

It's getting harder to get away with hypocrisy these days. We may think that we have privacy or are invulnerable to small-town gossip, but it's now a YouTube world, where someone can catch our behavior on a cell phone and upload it for all the world to see in minutes. This makes it harder for any of us to live without integrity and continue to delude ourselves, yet it's extraordinary to watch people on television adamantly denying something they said or did that's all over the Internet and has been viewed by millions of people.

It can actually be helpful to see ourselves on video because when we do, it's much harder to maintain the illusion that we aren't rigid, smug, or insecure. By the same token, we tend to have difficulty looking at pictures of ourselves because the images often contradict our impressions about how we appear. The extra weight, the wrinkles, the strained looks, and the body language that says "I'm not happy" are much harder to deny when we're observing ourselves in a photograph.

You don't need mirrors, photos, and embarrassing YouTube videos to reflect your behavior back to you; simply look at the evidence and listen to those who are dropping clues that you're not acting in sync with your intent. Be aware of what you're doing, whether it's driving like you own the road or insisting, "Oh, no problem, I'm not mad," when you're secretly seething with resentment.

Remember to Live in Integrity

As you can see, acting with emotional and moral courage means being true to your values. To live in integrity, you have to be clear on what those values are. Perhaps you were raised with a rigid set of rules about right and wrong and were quite shocked the first time you stepped out of your neighborhood or comfort zone and met someone with entirely different values.

To illustrate what I mean, I'd like to tell you a story of when I was a young man exploring the Amazon. Some friends and I were hosted by a group of rain-forest dwellers who provided us with a great feast, which we understood to be their way of thanking us for the gifts we'd brought for them.

One girl of about 12 was so gracious to one of my companions that even when he retired to his tent for the night, she kept stopping by, offering to come in and give him fresh water or anything else he might need. He became so unsettled by her continual attention that he finally went out, woke up the guide we'd hired, and asked him, "What's going on? Why is this kid constantly trying to wait on me?" The guide spoke to some villagers and returned with the news that we'd just attended a wedding feast—and surprise! The groom was my pal.

My friend and I were in utter shock at the thought that by indulging in this feast, he'd accidentally married this girl! We packed up in the middle of the night and rushed our group out of there. Afterward, we felt so bad for the humiliation we must have caused the poor girl that we paid for her to attend school at a nearby village. More than a decade later, I ran into her and discovered that she'd remarried, had borne several children, and was now a liaison between her people and outsiders, thanks to the language skills and education she'd received as a result of our support.

In my world, marrying off a 12-year-old to a stranger was unthinkable, so it never dawned on me that by having this particular feast with the natives, my friends and I were agreeing to a marriage. Yet as an anthropologist, I also realize that every culture has values that it assumes are held by everyone else, and it can be tricky to interact with people who live by a very different set of rules. Therefore, when practicing truth, the aim is to always act in a way that's congruent with our values *and* respectful of others'.

To avoid the discomfort of discovering that our values are different from other people's, we often choose to stick with our own kind. It gives us comfort to live in a neighborhood where we can boldly state our opinion and know that no one we encounter will contradict us and express a different view. When our ideals are questioned, or we meet someone whom we find pleasant and kind but who admits to having completely different ones, we experience shock and outrage. For example, we take for granted the value of democracy and believe that it's the best type of government for everyone in the world—and we're up in arms when a Middle Eastern country decides that it wants to live ruled by Islamic law.

If we're honest with ourselves, we're challenged to question our own dogma. Yet we often resist experiencing this painful conflict, deciding instead to be true to the values we were raised with . . . even when they don't work for us (that's why the rule in our culture is "Never discuss politics or religion"). It's easier not to have to wrestle with what we believe unconsciously or face the fact that we aren't always in sync with the people we love and care about.

I remember once having dinner with the mythologist Joseph Campbell, and he shared over a glass of wine that "what we call reality are only those myths that we have not quite seen through yet." However, to be emotionally and morally courageous, we need to set aside our personal truth, which is not always agreed upon by others, and practice universal truth.

Practice Universal Truth

There's a narcissistic notion in our culture that as long as we're in touch with our own truth and are speaking it, we have a certain level of nobility. We focus on our right to be honest, forgetting that everyone has a personal truth that's equally valuable—or equally meaningless. Practicing personal truth is a poor substitute for practicing universal truth. Not only is the former not very creative, it also only serves to justify the story of a rescuer, bully, or victim.

Every great spiritual tradition speaks about a universal truth that can be experienced by all, whether it's known as the "perennial philosophy" or "the Logos." A personal truth, on the other hand, is always a lie designed to justify the terror felt in the face of the mystery of creation. If my truth is different from yours, it's because we're both latching on to a limited idea, mistaking our own perspectives for the universal truth. The minute we become attached to our personal dogma, we start justifying it, and that's when we slip into the nightmare of disempowering stories.

If we were to drop our personal truths, we'd stop judging others according to what works for us. The "mommy wars" would end, and we'd cease comparing our global footprints and complaining about how the other guy isn't doing his fair share to save the planet. Americans tend to respond to the charge that we're being wasteful or insensitive by pointing fingers at some other group or country who's more wasteful or insensitive than we are. Of course we never point to anyone who's *less* wasteful or *more* sensitive than we are, since that would force us to be honest about our own failings. By griping about how much carbon China is putting into the atmosphere or how violent the terrorists are, we justify our own polluting, violent policies. Yet none of this contributes to a cleaner, safer world for anyone.

Personal truth is rooted in jaguar consciousness, which keeps us focused on what we think is "the" truth when it's only our perspective. In a relationship, a man might say, "You made a commitment to me but didn't follow through and stay in the relationship, so you've betrayed me"; this justifies his perception that his partner is a bully who victimized him. She, on the other hand, might feel that she was disrespected and unappreciated in the relationship, so her truth is that she's the victim while he's the bully. The universal truth is that both partners were so caught up in their psychological, karmic baggage that one of them chose to end the relationship. If they realized this higher truth, they'd be able to celebrate and thank each other for the lessons and the journey.

A universal truth doesn't have strong emotions and judgments attached to it the way a personal truth does. The universal truth about global warming, for instance, is that human beings are taxing the planet en masse, so they need to curb the activities that contribute to killing the earth. The universal truth about peace is that human beings routinely engage in acts of emotional, verbal, and physical violence; when confronted, they often make excuses for themselves.

The way to peace is through the practice of universal truth—it takes us out of the story of who's the good guy and who's the bad guy, and it helps us dream courageously and creatively instead of judging each other. But such truth can only be experienced and practiced through soul courage.

Practice Truth Through Soul Courage

With soul courage, we're aware of every opportunity to express and create truth, and we seize upon it. Our truth expresses itself in our actions and words; if we listen to what we say and the messages our bodies give us, we'll notice when we've slipped into the lie *and* the nightmare.

If you're courageously dreaming, you'll find that your language is active because courage is active. Describing yourself with pleasant adjectives, such as "caring" or "a spiritual, compassionate person," is a way of avoiding the challenge of engaging in caring, spiritual, compassionate action. Similarly, just as any man can become a "father," actual *fathering* is far more difficult to do. And being a lover is one thing, but courageously loving, and acting lovingly toward your partner of 20 years is something else.

Perhaps you've been caring, spiritual, and compassionate in the past and will be so in the future—but keep in mind that it's human nature to want to hang on to past laurels, regardless of whether they fit today. So confess to your desire to think of yourself as a good person, along with your habit of brushing aside the evidence that you're not behaving very well in the moment. Acknowledge the excuses you make for yourself, and practice truth.

When you dream courageously, your language will make it clear who's performing an action. Instead of complaining, "*Something* ought to be done about that situation," you'll say, "*I* ought to do something about that situation. *I* ought to dream up something

149

better and start making it happen." With the enormous creativity and passion of the soul, you'll recognize what action to take, and you'll step into your courage without hesitation.

It takes moral and intellectual valor to admit when we're hiding behind words to avoid being honest, ethical, courageous, or creative; or when we're using language to script stories. In war, we talk about "collateral damage" to civilians, speaking of our "freedom fighters" and "sharpshooters" trying to defeat the other side's "terrorists" and "snipers." Even the military has changed the name of its Sniper School to Sharpshooter School.

A client of mine told me she realized that she'd finally gotten over her story of victimhood when she changed her answer to the question "So what do you do?" Instead of beginning with "I'm a single mother" and following with a description of her woes, she now said, "I'm working on my master's degree in creative writing and raising two children," focusing on the actions she was taking in alignment with her intent.

In other words, what you think you *are*—a single mother, an entrepreneur, a cancer patient—is not necessarily a description of what you're doing today. You may be learning, exploring, healing, creating, or discovering. Break away from the simple labels you affix to yourself, discover what you're doing, and investigate if you'd rather try something different. Do be mindful that what you're doing is congruent with who you truly are.

Don't Forget the Humor!

Humor can be a powerful tool for practicing truth because it makes it much easier to handle harsh facts about our lives and to see ourselves clearly. That's why in the Middle Ages, the court jester was the one person in the kingdom who could tell the king the uncomfortable truth. When we're able to laugh at ourselves, we're drawing upon our courage. Our willingness to poke fun at ourselves also inspires others to let go of their masks and practice truth.

However, cynical humor can also be used to avoid the truth. Practicing truth means valuing and respecting all people: Jokes that are meant to intimidate or hurt someone else lock you into a disempowering story of being a righteous bully. Jokes meant to reassure another or lift them up, on the other hand, are refreshing and disarming. Laughter allows you to take the drama out of a situation and alleviates the sting of honesty. The legend of the Laughing Buddha says that he achieved enlightenment by capturing venomous snakes and removing their fangs so that they could harm no one. Truth, tempered by laughter, heals.

Humor lets you see that you've gotten stuck in the script for a bad movie or soap opera; it reminds you that you can come up with something more empowering than "I've just been betrayed by my best friend" or "My doctor gave me a grim prognosis and took away all my hope." With humor, you see the glass as half full (or even just a quarter full) because it connects you to a sense of optimism and positivity. Instead of being the lone cowboy riding off into the sunset, you become one of those who has risen from the ashes of a relationship or conquered the fear of death and loss.

Remarking, "This is going to make a great story when it's all over," or "I feel like we're in the world's worst reality show here" allows you to laugh along with everyone else in the lifeboat. It also reminds you that the facts of any situation are always changing, so as soon as you alter the way you see those facts, you begin to change reality. Even in the darkest situations, humor that expresses your ability to dream a better world brings in the light.

Laughter helps repair our bodies of tension's wear and tear, decreases levels of the stress hormone *cortisol,* protects our heart, and strengthens immunity. And there's no doubt that the universe itself has a sense of humor, and laughter is written into our DNA. In fact, in Hinduism, the sacred syllable *Om* is said to be the sound of the universe laughing.

Everyday life can be absurd, filled with evidence that the Creator has a sense of whimsy. As they say, if you want to make God laugh, tell Him your plans.

Partners in Practicing Truth

Most of us have at least one person in our lives, often a family member or an old friend, who keeps us honest by refusing to go along with any of our delusions. We gripe about them, avoid them, threaten to end the relationship . . . and then find ourselves irresistibly drawn to interact with them. Ultimately, we have to admit that we're attracted to their company because they won't let us get away with our dishonesty. It can be painful when someone is too blunt with us, but most of us instinctively hold on to the person whom we can always count on to tell us when we're getting a big head, not being true to ourselves, or not acting in sync with what we say is our intent.

Such a "nudge" can be very useful in helping you regularly practice the truth. You can always make the choice to train others to communicate with you in a more gentle way, but do value those individuals' honesty and have the courage to thank them for it.

Too often, therapists collude in our disempowering stories and sweetly remind us of how trapped we are in the past, confirming, "Well, you know, you *are* an adult child of an alcoholic, so of course you're drawn to men who mistreat you." Good counselors, however, will also be nudges, gently but firmly insisting that we practice truth, saying, "I know that your father was an abusive alcoholic and you've been drawn to men who mistreated you in the past—but where is the payoff here in going out with someone you just met who told you flat out that he has problems being loyal in relationships?"

The nudge will also remark, "You're drinking again? I thought you said you gave that up." She's the young daughter who mirrors all your unresolved issues and blithely says, "Well, I don't see why I can't do it if you're allowed to do it," challenging you to come up with a logical explanation for your pretense.

In the following exercise, you'll get practice in letting go of avoidance behaviors and start to become your own nudge.

Exercise: Becoming Your Own Nudge

We like to believe that we're true to our values at all times, but the fact is that most of us have betrayed our deepest principles mere seconds after self-righteously insisting that we'd never, ever violate them. It's like the story of the scorpion and the turtle who meet at the edge of the river. The scorpion asks the turtle to take him across the water on his back. "I would gladly do so," the turtle responded, "but I know that you'll probably sting me."

The scorpion says that of course he wouldn't; since he can't swim, if he stung the turtle in the middle of the river, they'd both die. The turtle agrees that this makes sense, and allows the scorpion to climb onto his back. Halfway through the crossing, the scorpion stings him in the neck, and the stunned turtle cries, "Why did you do that?" As they both begin to sink, the scorpion replies, "It's my nature."

Try to articulate your loftiest goal for yourself: Do you aspire to be a great healer, end poverty in your lifetime, or use the music you create to convince countless people to see love all around them? Even if you realize that your ambition sounds grandiose, don't judge yourself. Allow yourself to be extravagant for the moment.

Now ask yourself what your dream is, without all the ego-driven goals attached to it. Could it be that it's to work at healing others and yourself or to do whatever you can to alleviate the suffering of impounded dogs in your neighborhood? Is your dream to express yourself through music and perhaps influence others to practice music themselves? Remember that your dream shouldn't be to reach an end point of mastery and power; it should be something you can accomplish today in a small moment.

Close your eyes and imagine what you might do to manifest that vision before you retire tonight. If you choose to make a long-term goal—such as booking a meditation-retreat weekend for six months from now, or planning a vacation at an amusement park to spend some quality time with your children—that's fine, but break it down now. How can you meditate today, before you go to bed?

How can you spend quality time with your children today, even if it's on the phone, before they fall asleep?

Now that you know what you want to do, and you realize that your dream is fueled by the passion of your soul rather than the will of your ego, find a way to act courageously before the day ends. You might choose to speak an uncomfortable truth that serves to repair a relationship or interact in a new way with someone in order to create a deeper sense of intimacy with them. Whatever your inventive and courageous act, do it now.

≈ ≈ ≈

Being mindful and nonjudgmental and practicing universal truth are all necessary if you want to dream a better reality. They lay the foundation for the next Earthkeeper practice: Clean up your river.

~~~~~

CHAPTER EIGHT

Clean Up Your River

Do. Or do not. There is no try.
— YODA

Our lives are like flowing rivers: When we try to control their course, we merely flail about until we're swept under the waters that are heavy with silt, which is the toxic residue of our psychological and karmic wounding. Having no idea how to clean the silt up, we drink it in, and it chokes us—leaving us thirsting for a clean, clear stream to help us thrive.

We fight the current, yet we never clean the river. That is, we continue to attract people and situations that mirror our toxicity. We find that the more angry we are, the more we have to be angry about. The more abandoned we feel, the more we're attracted to others who abandon those they care about.

Unfortunately, none of our struggling helps us in the slightest. We're eventually left with nothing living in our river: no dreams, no hopes, no love, no passion, and no self-respect. And our waters don't bring life to anything on our shores, so the end result is a dead zone around us where nothing flourishes.

It's time to recognize the origin of those polluting elements and shut off the source.

Western psychology tells us that we have to install sewage-treatment plants and filtration systems to make our water drinkable once again. For the Earthkeepers, nothing could be further from the truth: They believe that the river cleans itself once we start feeding it crystalline water rather than pumping poisons into it. Then we can go with the flow wherever it takes us, trusting that the river knows what the best destination for us is. Once our waters flow clean, we don't have to search for our destiny; it's been there all along, waiting for us to turn our river into a stream of nourishment and passion.

Practice Beauty

When you start pouring beauty into your river, you'll find that the waters are becoming clearer every day. For example, the people who used to push your buttons will drift away—when you meet someone who would have irritated you in the past, you'll feel no desire to engage in battle with them. Likewise, you'll lose interest in venting and be unmotivated to whip up anger or outrage. The situations that you once found overwhelmingly depressing or infuriating will simply become situations. You won't judge them as good or bad, or empowering or crippling, because you'll know that facts are always in a state of flux, even when it looks as if they're static. You'll remember that your life will arrange itself to mirror your healthy, unpolluted condition.

To practice beauty, you must give up the ugly stories in which someone is a victim and someone else is the perpetrator. You must stop seeing the world through gray-smudged glasses, declaring that everyone and everything is coming up short of your expectations. You have to let go of cynicism and apathy and find hope and possibility in all people and situations.

This is especially hard to do in a culture that greatly values clever expressions of cynicism and declares that ugliness is truth, and the truth is ugly. Talk-show hosts, political pundits, and snide bloggers all revel in their ability to expose the "truth" about how no one can be trusted, there's nothing to believe in, and all of our heroes are actually fools and frauds. Soon we find ourselves thinking this way, too, finding conspiracies everywhere. Believing in beauty starts to seem naïve and childish rather than wise and refreshingly childlike. Our river becomes so thick with stories about good guys and bad guys that we can't see the bottom for all the muck.

Practicing beauty means recognizing what is pure and of value in every situation and every person. It means that even when your neighbor has done you a terrible wrong and is full of venom, you still love him as yourself, for you see in him the potential for being a better person and the part that was once a loving child. (You may have to squint very, very hard to discover such beauty amidst the ugliness, but it is always there, in any human.) You may have to guard yourself from your neighbor until such time as he's able to see that beauty in himself and begin acting in a beautiful way. Nevertheless, the moment you choose to see beauty is the moment you empower yourself to rise above the ugliness and let go of the stories that are clogging your river.

Remember Your Jaguar Courage

Our culture has urged us to take personal responsibility for ourselves and our woes . . . even as it encourages us to feel victimized, blame our condition on others, and remain in the same unhealed state. It's not that we don't aspire to be responsible, healthy individuals; it's just that we're bombarded by messages telling us that the solution to our troubles is to go ahead and obtain some product, service, or ideology to make us feel better. In the meantime, we point the finger of blame at other people and remain in our victim mode. From our insistence that our parents didn't give us enough of what we needed to our notion that it's the fault of Middle Eastern terrorists that our world is no longer a safe place, we maintain the attitude that someone else is the problem.

The more we listen to the message that we're not really responsible for our situations, the more tempted we are to start spinning yarns about our victimhood and reaching for a quick fix instead of practicing beauty, which takes great courage at the level of jaguar. We have to let go of our dogma about how things are and instead open ourselves to the possibility that the facts have changed, so our hypothesis needs to be revised. We have to release the strong emotions that drive our stories of victimhood and compel us to be noble rescuers and bullies.

In America, we're so mesmerized by our feelings that we practically worship them. We confuse the reality in our mind—our personal reality—with *all* reality, mistaking our personal truth for universal truth, and we come to believe that our feelings and notions are of the utmost importance. Since our minds create our impressions of reality, this can create a real problem when we use our negative emotions and thoughts to script disempowering stories. If we choose instead to access the emotional, moral, and intellectual courage available to us at the level of jaguar consciousness, we'll propel ourselves out of those old, paralyzing stories. Jaguar courage helps us to begin cleaning our river and practicing beauty.

A client of mine was deeply hurt when her husband didn't visit her in the hospital after she had an operation. His excuse was that hospitals made him uncomfortable with all their unfamiliar smells and sick people, and he told his wife he felt he needed to "honor" his feelings of discomfort and not subject himself to being in a sick bay. Her needs didn't factor in to his decision, since his own were monumentally important to him.

Had this man opened up to jaguar courage, he would have set aside his feelings and found beauty in his ability to sit next to his wife and give her comfort. He would have appreciated that she was being cared for and getting well, and he would have been grateful that he could be there to express his support for the woman he loved. He wouldn't have been distracted by the smells, sounds, and sights of the hospital—or the drama of his feelings. Unfortunately, he wasn't able to do any of this.

Indulging in our emotions, obsessing about why we feel the way we do, and applauding ourselves for devoting so much time to self-exploration can be just as paralyzing as being unaware of why we feel and act the way we do. Self-reflection serves its purpose, and all emotions—even the most uncomfortable ones—are valuable because they can clue us in to the stories we're telling ourselves, waking us up out of the nightmare and reminding us to start dreaming again. The problem is that our fascination with our own neuroses and emotions can cause us to become caught in a quagmire of self-reflection, acting cowardly, and ignoring others, just like in the Greek myth of Narcissus.

According to the legend, Narcissus was a handsome but self-absorbed youth who rejected all those who would offer him love, until a spurned lover became angry at his selfishness and cursed him with the fate of experiencing unrequited love. Narcissus caught sight of himself in a pool, fell madly in love with his reflection, and leaned in to kiss it—and was heartbroken when his "beloved" broke up into ripples. He sobbed in grief but then noticed that his beloved had returned to the river. Joyously, he tried to kiss his reflection again, only to have it dissolve once more. Alas, once the water settled again, he had to accept that he could never in fact touch the one he loved, so he sat on the shore gazing longingly at his reflection, pining away in sorrow until he finally died.

Like Narcissus, we can become caught up in our endless thoughts about ourselves, insisting that the perfect situation will present itself in the future and there's no need to "settle" for what's being offered to us now. If we're constantly rejecting opportunities because we're so focused on beliefs such as *I'm worthy of something far better than this,* then we'll be cursed to spend our days contemplating the same old boring questions of *Who am I? Why am I here?* We'll be left waiting for the day when our life arranges itself to meet with our expectations of perfection. Of course that day will never come, and we'll be stuck on the shore of the pond staring at our own reflection.

Being honest about your own failings and character flaws—setting aside your shame, embarrassment, and defensiveness—is a great beginning to cleaning up your river, but it's only a beginning. Accept that your river is polluted, but don't get stuck making excuses, such as "Well, that's just how I am; people simply have to accept me." No spiritual teacher, therapist, devoted spouse, or child is going to clean the river for you. Only you can do it.

The True American Way

We become overly fascinated by our stories and emotions as a culture. We wonder who we are as Americans, for instance, and what our character is. We'll discuss ourselves endlessly rather than moving from analysis to action. As a nation, we could be changing the way we treat our most vulnerable citizens (as well as those of other countries), but we're too busy being obsessed with our dogmas and values, which we claim are the best in the world.

We say that freedom is so important that it's worth any cost, even if that cost is global warming, the exploitation of poor people, and depletion of the planet's resources. As long as we're allowed to buy the big house, the gas-guzzling car, and the fast-food hamburger, we're willing to pass along the cost to others, regardless of whether it's our grandchildren or inhabitants of underdeveloped countries. If we really believed that freedom is a vitally important universal value, we'd honor and value other people's right to breathe clean air, drink unpolluted water, and live their lives their own way without our trying to fix them. We'd let go of our stories and find the beauty in their way of life.

The United States has a secret and uncomfortable history of invading other countries and browbeating them into following our lead. We've overthrown governments and installed dictators we thought would look out for our business interests (Noriega in Panama, the Shah in Iran, and so on), reasoning that everyone would benefit through some sort of trickle-down process. We forget that the most effective ways to share democracy and liberty is by being patient, respecting others, and modeling all that we truly value, not through bullying and behaving self-righteously. We violate the principles of democracy in order to impose it on others, and then we're confused when they reject our form of government.

Over the course of history, those who have been influenced by the U.S. were less impressed by our rhetoric than by our courageous actions and our examples of generosity and creativity. In fact, some of the greatest American innovations haven't come from the desire to generate profit alone but from the desire to explore, discover, and be creative. The original intention of the Walt Disney Company, for example, was to bring magic into the hearts of children all over the world. Mr. Disney and his animators put their hearts and souls into creating groundbreaking movies such as *Fantasia,* which didn't make money for years.

Similarly, the blues and jazz artists of the 1920s and the great rock and rollers of the 1950s and 1960s weren't trying to build security for themselves by adhering to a proven formula for success. And neither Bill Gates nor Steve Jobs ensured that they had the security of college degrees before dreaming of personal computers in every home and tinkering in a garage to make their dream come true.

When we Americans live and act according to our principles, we inspire others. In all corners of the world, people are influenced by our music and technology. Our symbols of liberty have been used by the French in their Revolution and the Chinese in their Tiananmen Square protest in 1989. So as a country, we have more to offer the planet than the promise of a McDonald's or Starbucks on every main street from Bangkok to Paris. And as individuals, we impress the rest of the world when we walk our talk instead of saying, "Do as I say, not as I do."

Jaguar courage lets us all examine our actions and remove hypocrisy from the river. We buy into our own disempowerment as long as we continue endlessly and fruitlessly analyzing ourselves, giving tremendous weight to our feelings and our stories; blaming others for our problems; and fretting about why love, peace, contentment, and acceptance don't magically appear in our lives and around the globe. Even if we guess that we're attracting the people and situations that aren't making us happy, our focus on trying to figure out why we feel the way we do gives so much attention to our fears and insecurities that we breathe life into them. Then we get stuck coming up with more and more stories of victimhood and bemoaning our powerlessness instead of dreaming courageously.

Use Your Superpowers

Knowing the source of our stories helps us identify the toxins that are poisoning our river and cutting us off from our passion, but that's only the first step. Unfortunately, many of us never take the next one, in which we realize that *we're* that source. And we start to recognize how we repeat our old tales like a songwriter whose music all starts to sound the same as she recycles the same tired riffs.

If you're stuck in a story you've titled "How Could I Have Married That Idiot?" own your power to tell the story differently—then choose, consciously, to construct a new one immediately. Here in your courageous dream, you're reborn as a heroic survivor with a past that reveals the source of your wisdom and power. The years you spent suffering physical and emotional abuse during your marriage, for instance, tempered you and taught you how to be compassionate. You didn't learn about compassion from reading the Dalai Lama's book; you learned it in the lion's mouth. Your new story will allow you to find the beauty in your failed marriage and even in your former spouse. It will give you the courage to thank him or her for the lessons he or she taught you, no matter how painful it was to learn them.

In comic books, superheroes usually start off as ordinary people who acquire amazing powers after something terrible happens to them: Their parents are killed, they're bitten by a radioactive spider, or they're blasted in a rocket away from their exploding home planet. The tragedy marks the beginning of their new lives as heroes with extraordinary abilities and great courage they never had before.

In the following exercise, you can discover your own heroic origins and claim your powers.

Exercise: The Action Hero

Think about a tragic event you've experienced, and then construct a narrative about it that doesn't cast blame on you or anyone else. Tell the story in the third person, describing the dramatic experience as something that simply happened, a turn in your tale that sets up the listener to understand how you developed your extraordinary gifts.

Remember, you are the storyteller, and in the moment you tell a new story with power and conviction, you make it begin to come true. To that end, explain why your divorce, abandonment, illness, suffering, or loss gave you abilities you'd never had before. What are your acquired powers? Can you now "fly" above your everyday woes? Do you have "x-ray vision" that allows you to see through people, observing what others cannot? Can you stretch yourself like Plastic Man or fend off bullets with your golden bracelets and quick reflexes like Wonder Woman?

Unlike in the comic books, you don't have to write about being alienated or misunderstood because of your differentness. In your personal storybook, you can surround yourself with other heroes who have their own unique gifts. You can inspire others with your fearlessness but also have your off days when you rely on the others around you to help as you regroup.

As you write your tale, in your head or on paper, imagine what you might do today with your powers to manifest truth, justice, and freedom in your life. Don't imagine yourself to be a noble rescuer of the people of Gotham City, but rather a humble hero who accepts her destiny and fends off toxic beings by using her amazing gifts. Then leave your own batcave or fortress of solitude and let your courage express itself in your world today.

Clean Up Your Toxins Using Intellectual Courage

As you'll recall, intellectual courage is the audacity to be open to new ideas, question your dogma, and treat your accumulated knowledge as mere hypothesis. Whatever you think you know, test it out, again and again. Maybe today you'll discover that what you know to be true isn't so at all, or it is true but only in certain circumstances.

When the Aztecs settled in central Mexico, they inherited a prophecy about the return of "the Lord of the Dawn," a man-god who would bring about a great upheaval and then lasting peace and abundance to all. Around the time indicated by the prophecy, Aztec scouts spied huge ships with great billowing white sails coming from the east, the place of the dawn. The arriving conquistadors were received as gods by the Aztecs . . . who then got to witness the devastation of their cities and way of life thanks to these "gods." Their priests were so wedded to their notion of the "truth" that they failed to recognize the greatest peril faced by the indigenous peoples of the Americas. Yet this doesn't mean that the truth of their prophecy was flawed, only their take on the timing. They simply failed to test their hypothesis against reality.

One of the ways we become trapped in stories is through the creation of beliefs that we live by as if they were written in stone. Some forms of therapy, such as cognitive behavioral therapy, can help us step back from our beliefs, analyze them objectively, and recognize how limiting our "knowledge" or views are. We can discover just how distorted our perceptions are when we examine the words that come out of our mouths.

For example, when my kids were little and I wouldn't let them do something, they'd complain that I *never* let them have any fun, and that I was *always* denying them what they wanted. I'm sure that felt true for them at the time, but as I'd remind them, I'd just taken them to the video arcade, let them stay up late to watch a movie, or indulged them in some other way. Of course they'd forgotten all of this the moment I denied them something.

Even as adults, we don't recognize when we're distorting our perceptions to conform to our feelings of the moment: We insist that "no one" has ever truly loved us, that "everyone" undervalues us, and that we "never" get our way. Our language of extremes—*always, never, no one, everyone*—betrays how skewed our perceptions can be. We load up our minds with all sorts of faulty thoughts that we mistake for indelible facts: *I know I'll never have the sort of financial security my parents did because our economy has been totally screwed up,* or *There's no one out there for me—I'll never find love.*

Our peers encourage us to buy into the common "knowledge" that may or may not be true for us today, locking us into rigid, dogmatic beliefs, such as:

- Men seek freedom, while women seek intimacy and connection.

- Sex and romance die after marriage.

- It's all downhill after high school.

- Retirement is the beginning of irrelevancy.

- Technology can solve any problem.

Many of my clients are facing health crises and ominous prognoses, and I've found that there are two common responses to this dire news. Either they'll launch a deep spiritual journey into understanding why they're here on this earth, having this experience, and ultimately learn the lessons the illness is here to teach them; or they'll immerse themselves in the language and activities of the medical community, analyzing their lab results from day to day, and focusing all their attention on their health care.

Members of the latter group sometimes come to me expecting a miraculous cure. I have to explain to them that health is the result of a lifestyle, and so is healing, so they must work with their physicians as well as their shaman to craft a new story of wellness at a physical, emotional, and spiritual level.

In fact, I tell all of my clients that I'll only work with them with energy medicine if they're willing to see and work with a Western-medicine doctor as well, as it's important to address health on all levels. Yet I also believe that too often, people put all their faith in the story that Western medicine can address their illness and recovery. They desperately want to believe that technology can solve any problem, so they hang their hopes for recovery on a new procedure or test that seems promising. Yes, the procedure may help, but having the intellectual courage to say, "Maybe this is something that technology alone can't solve" can open them up to other ways of healing that they may have been closed off to.

We urge citizens to learn CPR and stock defibrillators in airports and public schools just in case someone has a heart attack—although few people realize that even in the best of circumstances, CPR and a properly used defibrillator will only save a small percentage of heart-attack victims. We want to believe that with the right tool, we can fix anything—after all, that's how it works in the movies and on TV. When Western medicine and its fancy machines don't prevent someone from dying, we find it devastating that our knowledge, and our technology, have failed us.

≈ ≈ ≈

With intellectual courage, you can question all you know about what can "never" occur, what "always" happens, what "everyone" knows and does, and what "no one" will ever understand or accept. You can recognize the cultural myths you've accepted unquestioningly, which have kept you trapped in a nightmare, and begin to reconsider them. Then you can open yourself up to possibilities that the universe presents to you and step into the flow of your river.

You don't want to get stuck endlessly analyzing yourself and becoming enthralled by the workings of your psyche and emotions. What's important is to let go of judgments about yourself, others, and your situation—simply observe it all with curiosity. When you access intellectual courage, you can start thinking anew about what you're doing and why events are unfolding as they are. What lessons might the universe be nudging you to learn?

Let go of fear and become curious, allowing yourself to think of the possibilities inherent in a situation. Find the beauty that's hidden beneath the story known as "I Have a Problem"; it might be the opportunity to create deeper intimacy with your partner as you heal together from a loss, or the chance to develop better communication with your child after you discover that he's started smoking pot. Then you'll achieve equanimity, a balance of thoughts and feelings in the mind, and be able to express jaguar courage more easily.

Practicing beauty and jaguar courage is easier to do when you take time out to be quiet and reflective because it's difficult to retain composure in the presence of strong words or emotions—be they yours or someone else's. Make a mistake when you're driving and you're likely to experience another driver shouting at you and calling you an idiot (or worse). Notice what happens when someone honks their horn at you: You immediately respond to accommodate them, or else you think that you're doing something wrong. It takes courage to let go of your feelings of nervousness, anger, or embarrassment; or of thoughts such as *I'm a terrible, dangerous driver* or *This road is far too confusing for me to handle* or *Judgmental jerk! I'll show him!*

Intellectual courage allows you to take a deep breath and step back from negative, distorted myths such as *Anybody who cuts others off on the road is a self-centered, malicious bastard;* you're able to recognize that while this may sometimes be true, it's not the only possible explanation for another person's behavior. Sometimes after you've experienced such an upsetting incident, it's best to take a moment afterward to regain your perspective and remind yourself how hard it is to reject the old stories when you're under pressure.

Once I was driving with a friend, who is a renowned healer, into Los Angeles. We got stuck in a monumental traffic jam, making him late for an appointment, so he called his client and they agreed to have their session on the phone. I decided to close my eyes and follow along as he guided this man through a meditation, bringing love and forgiveness to each organ in his client's body.

I was being lulled into a pleasant trance by my friend's voice, when for some reason I opened my eyes and noticed him flipping off the guy in the next car for cutting in front of him. He was mouthing "F - - k you" silently, without skipping a beat of the guided meditation with his client.

I'd just moved to L.A. at that time and wasn't yet familiar with the ways of road rage common in Southern California. So imagine my surprise when at the end of the session, while we were still inching forward in traffic, my friend turned to me and explained, "That's just the way we connect with each other here in L.A.—it's no big deal, really." With time, I understood that road rage is merely a form of sport to many Californians, and that you develop high blood pressure only when you take such exchanges seriously.

In the following exercise, you'll learn to question some thoughts and beliefs that you take for granted. Examining what you believe to be the undisputable truth will help you discover that it's only your personal reality.

Exercise: Upside Down

Identify a situation or individual that annoys, upsets, and irritates you—that something or someone you prefer to avoid. Close your eyes and try to imagine the affirmative qualities about this circumstances or person. What could be positive about being caught in heavy traffic with aggressive drivers surrounding you? What's the upside of forgetting an important appointment and having to apologize to the person you were supposed to meet? What's the silver lining in getting laid off? What are the good qualities of that politician, celebrity, co-worker, or in-law whom you say you can't stand? What do you love and respect about the President you didn't vote for? Where is the beauty in a loss?

As you find the upside of that which makes you feel bad, imagine what other gifts are hidden in plain sight. What unnerving possibilities, difficult lessons, and uncomfortable reminders are you avoiding that could help you in your spiritual maturation process?

Next, identify something you love, admire, or are inspired by and then imagine what is ugly, unpleasant, and annoying about it. What bothers you about having a romantic partner who deeply loves you? What complaints do you have about your beautiful home? What's so irritating about a basket of adorable kittens?

(Understand that the point here is not to nurture pessimism but to recognize the shadow side of what gives you happiness.)

As you open yourself up to creativity and honesty, identify the downside of that which you love and appreciate—or have been told you should love and appreciate. Explore that downside, without judging yourself or feeling guilty for having negative feelings about something that "ought" to make you happy. When you identify what's being hidden in the shadows of your psyche and bring it into the light for examination, you can consciously choose to discard it, whether it's the thought that *Emotional intimacy is confining, and my relationship is holding me back from exploring all that life has to offer* or *I hate feeling that I have to constantly clean and redecorate my home.*

Have the courage to question your dogma, and commit to testing out your hypothesis. Today, is it true that intimacy is trapping you? Is it true that as a man, you don't have a strong need for emotional security in a relationship? Is someone else holding you back right now, or are you doing that all by yourself without anyone's help? What would happen if you let your house alone and spent your energy, time, and money on something other than landscaping and updating the "look" of your home?

By questioning your dogma or personal truth, and subsequently discovering your subconscious thoughts and feelings, you open yourself up to thinking creatively and dreaming courageously.

Clean Up Your Toxins Using Moral Courage

To finish cleaning up your river, you need to express moral courage, which means not just discerning what the right thing to do is but actually doing it. Simply recognizing the right thing to do can be difficult when you're caught in a jaguar mental nightmare. You can begin by letting go of resentment, judgment, and outrage; then ask yourself, "How can I honor this person's values as well as my own?" This allows you to let go of the distorted beliefs that lead to conflict, hurt, and resentment; and you'll be launched into hummingbird consciousness. The symbol of the hummingbird is important because this courageous little bird nourishes itself only on nectar and does not feed on bitterness, contradiction, or discord.

With moral courage, we take personal responsibility for our actions rather than simply paying lip service to our ideals. We tell others we're sorry, even if we think we were right. We know that an apology doesn't mean *I'm the bad guy and I did something wrong,* but *I offer you empathy because I see you're suffering.* With moral courage, we offer to make amends for any role we played in someone else's suffering. We don't defend our actions by saying, "Okay, so I did that, but what you did was even worse," or "It's not my problem you were offended by what I did." Moral courage allows us to create peace with ourselves and others.

With emotional courage, we love boldly in our intimate relationships. Keep in mind that all the romantic partners we've had came to us to help us heal and grow. When they were infuriating us and making us resentful, they were simply doing their job in the story we scripted.

All too often we turn our love partners into intimate enemies whom we hold responsible for our unhappiness and failures. Most experts agree that it takes about 24 months for romantic love to end and the heaven to turn into hell. Emotional courage requires us to *rise* rather than fall in love, becoming the authors of a heroic tale in which we stop searching for the next "right" partner and grow to be it ourselves. This type of courage means that we don't change the partner, but we do change our script of the relationship.

When you find the moral courage to let go of a defensive stance, don't expect instant absolution and release, and don't insist that the other person agree with your new story. Remember that *this* also is a story. Simply follow through on your vow to become the storyteller, and resist falling back on the old standby that you're the real victim, not him or her.

It's interesting that after an extramarital affair, the partner who betrayed his promise to be faithful will often be contrite and treat his lover with great tenderness, only to begin to resent that he hasn't been forgiven yet. Exasperated, he'll demand to know just when he can stop sleeping on the couch and when his partner will extend trust again, as if she should agree to a timetable for resentment and say, "Okay, as of the 15th of next month, I'll freely give you my love and faith again with no reservations. That seems like a fair sentence for your offense, don't you think?"

Of course, moral courage also requires the partner who's been let down to begin releasing that resentment rather than holding on to her story of being betrayed. Hurt, anger, and distrust are great emotions for awakening her compassion; but if she holds on to them, they'll become psychological wounds that doom her to keep re-creating situations that mirror her hurt, anger, or distrust.

Moral courage gives us the power to clean up our river by forgiving others as we forgive ourselves. We know from accounts of near-death experiences that after we pass from the physical world into the realm where time flows like a river, we'll have to relive every memory of harming, or being harmed by, another. We'll feel what the other people in our past experienced and finally be able to let go of the anger and resentment we feel toward them, even as we let go of our own guilt. However, this cleansing of the river can happen at any time.

When my father was very ill and clearly in his last days, for instance, he asked me to help him through the dying process. I told him to imagine sitting on a boulder that overlooked a stream that was filled with every memory of his life. It was difficult for him to do this at first, so I urged him to picture what transpired the first time he wore long pants, to recall an image of when he was a boy in the very first house he lived in, and so on. Visual memories came back to him, flowing like a river before him, and I walked him through the process of asking for forgiveness and forgiving others.

We performed this exercise several times over the course of two weeks, and I watched and listened as my father cried and spoke to the people in his memories, including himself. Finally, when he was finished making peace with every memory and person in his life, he passed away. I knew that he wouldn't have to clean up his river after death because he had already done so.

≈ ≈ ≈

The key to writing healing tales is the practice of beauty, for those without beauty can only bring suffering. This doesn't mean that we have to write stories with fairy-tale endings---it simply means that the stories we author and the endeavors we join in are guided by the principle of creating and bringing beauty to everyone involved. James Watson and Francis Crick, who discovered the molecular structure of DNA, were guided by the principle that whatever the most basic form of human life is, "it has to be beautiful." The Navaho poets wrote: "Beauty before me, beauty behind me, beauty all around me. In beauty I walk. . . ." A healing story has something exquisite within it.

With jaguar courage, you clean up your river by practicing beauty, by touching everyone and everything with that quality instead of with fear, anger, or trepidation. Then you'll notice that the waters in your river are becoming crystalline, that you can write volumes of loveliness and grace, and that you are the storyteller— not merely in the grip of your stories.

With soul courage, you can immerse yourself in the flow of your river, with full access to your passion for life. You accept that you're not in control of where your river flows, but only of how clean you keep its waters, and you learn to nourish yourself and others as you irrigate fields and pastures. Envision what your relationships would look like; think about how you'd interact with strangers in challenging situations, and in the small moments when fear threatens to pull you back into a lower state of consciousness and shut off your access to courage. Imagine what your world would be like if you let go of your dogma, your rigid beliefs, and your obsession with your own emotional responses to situations.

If you have the courage to practice beauty regardless of how difficult it seems to be, you'll clean up your river and let go of the fears that your ego creates. As you practice beauty, you'll find yourself ready to engage in the third Earthkeeper discipline: the practice of being ready to die at any moment.

~~~~~

CHAPTER NINE

Be Ready to Die at Any Moment

*He who fears death has
already lost the life he covets.*
— CATO THE CENSOR

The Earthkeepers believe that to live fully and dream courageously, we must wake up each morning and live this day as if it were our last. Only when we face the reality that we are mortal, and that we have no control over when we depart from this physical existence, do we find the courage to stop frantically running away from the death we fear and put our energy into living lives of originality and purpose.

To be ready to die at any moment requires great valor. We need the emotional courage to speak the truth now, to say to others what needs to be said, without delay. It's all too easy to tell ourselves, "Well, she knows I love her—I don't have to say it aloud" or "He knows I feel bad about our argument, but I'll clear the air later." We need moral courage so that we can align our behavior with our principles instead of making excuses for why it's all right to get back to acting from integrity later on, at a more convenient time.

With moral courage, we don't look at the mess we have made (or inherited but done nothing about), and say, "Let someone else figure out how to fix that problem." This brings to mind

Thomas Jefferson, who said before he died that he regretted that the Founding Fathers hadn't figured out how to solve the problem of slavery, which would now have to be addressed by future generations. We're still dealing with the fallout of generations of Americans who passed that problem along through Jim Crow laws, housing discrimination, and the like. With moral courage, we can be honest about what we're doing today that will shock our great-grandchildren the way we're shocked by the fact that our forefathers owned slaves, hunted species to extinction for the sport of it, and denied women the right to vote.

Being ready to die at any moment also requires the intellectual courage to let go of the old notions we inherited from our family, church, and culture about what we need to be happy. It means asking ourselves difficult questions such as, "Would I be content if I never got married or had kids, or if I never got to travel around the world? What if I follow my calling, but the consequence is that the one I love leaves me?"

Intellectual courage also means daring to change our minds about someone or something that we may take absolutely for granted. For example, it took great intellectual courage for Christopher Columbus to think that the world was not flat, as everyone else believed, and then follow his convictions. Many of us today continue to live in a "flat" world, with ideas and opinions that serve us well but limit our experience of reality.

Having the hummingbird courage to dream means following your calling today, in some way, despite the facts in your life that seem to be unmovable obstacles. It means not waiting until you've gathered all the materials—the financial nest egg, the wide-open blocks of time, and the understanding and support of those you care about—to begin dreaming. If your canvas is unfinished at the moment you die, at least you'll have died an artist instead of a daydreamer or dabbler who talks about how she'd truly like to live but only does so at odd moments here and there, such as when she's at a weekend retreat, momentarily inspired, or on vacation.

We procrastinate living the way we truly want because we think that we have all the time in the world for our dreaming to begin.

To that end, one of my closest friends made all sorts of plans for after he retired, working at a job he hated until he finally reached age 65 and could stop going to the office. Two months after this happened, he was dead, and his postponed dreams remained unfulfilled fantasies. His children seemed to have learned well from him, though, as they're using their small inheritance to travel around the world.

Remaining aware that death can come storming through our door at any time frees us from the type of death of the spirit that occurs when we put our dreaming ability on ice and simply slog through another day, hoping our lives will change for the better. The lifelessness that occurs when we're trapped in the nightmare is far worse than the one that occurs when we pass from this mortal existence into the next one. Yet in our culture we're oblivious to this death of the spirit because we're terrified of the death of the body. Fearing the end of our days, we try to stay frantically busy and keep it at bay.

The Illusion of Outwitting Death

Once upon a time in a Baghdad marketplace, there was a servant who bumped into Death himself. Terrified, the man dropped his purchases and ran home on foot. When he arrived, he breathlessly begged his master, "Please, may I borrow your fastest horse? I met Death in the marketplace, and he gestured like he was about to take me, so I ran back here as fast as I could. I must escape from him!"

The master said, "Take my fastest steed, and perhaps you can outrun Death tonight. Flee to Sammara, for he will never find you there." The servant thanked him profusely, and galloped off at breakneck speed toward the village of Sammara, which was many hours away.

The master then went to the marketplace, and when *he* saw Death, he asked, "Why did you threaten my poor servant when he was here earlier today?"

Death replied, "I wasn't threatening him. I was just shocked to see him, that's all. You see, I was expecting to meet up with him tonight—in Sammara."

Like the frightened servant, we desperately try to outrun our demise and deny its inevitability. We keep ourselves very busy, with an endless agenda of important tasks, reasoning that if we leave enough items pending, the end won't find us and interrupt our very significant work. "My company could never survive without me," we say, or "Everything would fall apart in this family if I weren't on top of it all." We can't bear to go to the corner to mail a letter without our cell phone in hand—if we're not available to other people every second of the day, we'd have to admit that the earth will indeed continue to rotate without us.

Fear of our death causes us to rush about here and there doing whatever we can to outwit it, only to feel trapped in our senseless existence. As Socrates said, "Beware the barrenness of a busy life." What we say are priorities don't even get penciled in on our to-do list. That quality time with our child or night out with our partner keeps getting postponed because we have to finish a report or go to the hardware store.

Often our justification for not dreaming is that we don't have enough time, money, or resources. These excuses are rooted in our fears at serpent and our stories at jaguar. What we really lack is not resources but the courage to say no to the nightmare and fears and tell the dream yes. This brings to mind my mother: When she turned 82, she told me that if she were younger she would have wanted to try bungee jumping, which sounded like a wonderful adventure to her.

I told her that there was a safer version of the sport she could try even at her age, called a zipline, involving a strong cable and a harness. My octogenarian mother was absolutely thrilled to be sent careening off a mountainside in Utah. Yet how often do most of us refuse to take any risks in life, even when we're young, because of our niggling fears?

We don't have to go into free fall with no cord attached, but we *can* jump into fully relishing life instead of trying to tiptoe in safety at all times. This makes me think of whenever one of my workshop participants comes up to me and exclaims, "I'm so glad I came! I've been reading your books and been meaning to do this for years." I always wonder what other life adventures they've been avoiding if they've taken years to muster the courage to step out of their comfort zone and begin their healing journey.

You may also be putting off living the way you'd like to live, becoming caught up in your everyday activities and your excuses for why you can't have the life you want. In the following exercise, you'll start imagining how you might make your dream manifest today, regardless of the obstacles you imagine.

Exercise: Your Perfect Day

What happens the moment you wake up in the morning: Do you leap out of bed to immediately start the day? If so, stay in bed a little longer next time to recall your dreams. Then, in that state of lucid reverie, visualize your perfect day. Imagine the people you interact with and the quality of your conversations. Hear yourself speaking truths that need to be spoken, as well as saying "I love you," "I forgive you," and "I'm sorry" to those you've been meaning to make amends to. See what you eat, where you are, and what happens before you fall asleep at night. Picture every detail.

Now ask yourself what you can do before this evening ends to experience every element of that perfect day, from the emotions you feel to the interactions and adventures you have. How can you bring the tropical beach into your world when it's bitterly cold outside? How can you play in the waves when you have to make dinner and return two dozen e-mails? Where is the relaxation, the whimsy and delight, and the communion with nature in your world right now?

Reject the notion that you have the rest of your life to plan and create this perfect day. Free yourself from the karmic baggage that's causing you to say you can't have the interactions and relationships you desire—the stuff that makes you feel that you can't risk getting hurt again or that you just don't have it in you to tolerate the ridicule you'd get if you were to step out and do what you really want. And get rid of the excuse that you don't have the money to fund your dream, and resources will flow in from unexpected sources once you set your intent in motion.

Discover the elements of your dream that are symbols of what you most love and value—and know that you can bring them into your life right now, wherever you are, whatever you're doing. Perhaps your perfect day takes place in Italy, where you're able to savor the experience of spending a lovely afternoon sitting on a veranda somewhere, drinking a fine wine and enjoying the lush gardens before your eyes. At hummingbird, you understand that you'll find a way to get there, literally or figuratively. You'll recognize that there will be cascading flowers, delights for the senses, and the exquisite luxury of time to enjoy it all, be it in Tuscany or in Toledo.

On the other hand, if you keep rushing about here and there, trying to scrape together enough cash to take your dream vacation, you may end up in Italy but you'll be disappointed. You'll find that the villa doesn't have wireless Internet capability, the wine is great but twice as expensive compared to what you can get at home, and the fantasy of the country reawakening your sensuality isn't coming to life like it does in one of those E. M. Forster novels. You'll decide that Italy is the problem, not your unwillingness to let go of your frenetic activity and surrender to the experience of sensual reawakening wherever you are in the world, regardless of what the facts of your life are. You won't truly live because you'll be too busy trying not to die.

Understand Which Death You Truly Fear

We think that we're afraid of death, but what we're really terrified of is the end of the ego, the self that we've come to know and love. Fearing that demise, we try to outrun it like the Baghdad servant did. Again, we do this by staying busy and pretending that we're too important to have our life plans interrupted. What we need to do instead is let go of our personal importance—of that self that has a particular set of memories, personality, and temperament that defines who we are—and identify with the soul that transcends death.

The courage to be ready to die at any moment comes from understanding that the self with personality, temperament, and memories (the ego self) is not your only self. You have an immortal self, and identifying with that rather than the ego takes tremendous courage. The more you identify with the soul and reside in hummingbird awareness, the easier it is to let go of your stories and shed the karma you've been carrying with you from lifetime to lifetime. You'll become lighter and more easily enter eagle consciousness, where "I" no longer exists as a separate entity. Eagle begins to feel like home, because it *is* home.

When we stop identifying with our personality, let go of our karma, and go home to the realm of the eagle, we cease fearing the death of the physical body and the end of our life on Earth. Knowing our immortal nature, we can remain immersed in the great ocean of infinity or be born again in human form for the purpose of learning or serving. Then we can become *avatars,* higher beings who deliberately come down into the earthly plane. Having transcended the soul itself, we will have attained the consciousness of the stars. As avatars, we'll have complete freedom to dream at a much higher level than that of the personal soul, and we can partake in the dreams of stars or even entire galaxies.

We can attain eagle consciousness in an instant, but it can take many lifetimes to get to that moment. The closest some of us will come is when we experience selfless love; here we taste infinity and use this new awareness to alleviate our fears of the unknown that await us after mortal death. Freed from this paralyzing fear of the ego's demise, we can participate in dreaming a world that benefits all in this lifetime, not just ourselves. I remember experiencing selfless love while holding my newborn son for the first time. For an instant or a lifetime, "I" disappeared, and all that existed was this child of life itself. As I dwelled in eagle consciousness, it was clear to me that I always resided there and did not need an outside stimulus like my son's birth to remind me how to get back "home."

Once you've experienced eagle, you'll never see things the same again. You'll be conscious of the fact that someone else will walk on the earth after you and that your actions will impact future generations. One of my clients, for instance, lives in an area where if there's too much water in the sewer system, the sewers will drain into the lake that's the water source for millions of people. He's careful to conserve water on rainy days, and he saves his laundry and car washing for times when using lots of water won't contribute to the pollution of the lake that he shares with his neighbors. He does all of this without any need to draw attention to his act or dub himself "the Noble Rescuer of the Lake" or "Good Citizen." He nurtures the lake just as he nurtures himself, because he understands that there is no "man" and "lake"—there is only Spirit expressing itself in the forms of "man" and "lake."

Having experienced eagle awareness, you can bring that wisdom back to the lower levels of perception and apply it to your daily life. Any sense of lack or of longing for something that remains out of reach will disappear. You'll be aware that your own river is part of a much greater one of infinity, which always flows pure and clean, and you'll decide that's the only water you want to drink from. Sparkling and clear, fertile and abundant with fish and reeds, your inner river will be flowing with plenty, nourishing the world.

Detaching from Your Roles

For most of us, our self-definition is so important that we cling to our labels and roles and never explore how we can redefine ourselves. Our roles are our ego; without them we feel that we'll be losing the essence of who we are and "dying."

In the following exercise, you'll incinerate your roles so that you can let go of their limitations. Afterward, you'll discover the possibilities of those roles without having to get stuck in the story you created around them. Your roles then become what you do instead of who you are. You can stop identifying with these roles at the level of jaguar, or mind, and discover their myriad possibilities at hummingbird, where any role can be discarded or transformed at any time because you're no longer identified with them.

Exercise: Burning Your Roles

To perform this exercise, you'll need some twigs, several strips of paper, a pen, a fire, and your soul's courage.

Gaze into the flames (which could be in a fireplace, barbecue, or fire pit), letting your thoughts slow down and fade in intensity. Cease to give them weight, and watch as they begin to dissipate. Fire has a mysterious ability of helping you enter the state of lucid reverie and access the dreamtime. Have you ever noticed how easy it is to spend hours by the fire without thinking or talking?

On each strip of paper, write a role, label, or self-definition that you identify with. Be sure to include *husband, wife, father, mother, doctor, breadwinner, nurse, recovering alcoholic, student, lover,* and so on. All of these roles, no matter how exalted, have bound you and kept you stuck in an uninspired nightmare. Nevertheless, wrap each strip around a twig, and thank each role for the lessons it has taught you and the powers it bestowed upon you. Bless each role, and then place the twig in the fire and watch it burn. Continue this process with all of your roles, and know that you're creating a sacred ritual for yourself without engaging the mind.

Feel the heat as each twig burns, making sure that you work from the level of hummingbird, of poetry and myth. Imagine the demands of your roles disappearing into smoke and ash, as you're freed from playing the part of mother, spouse, son, or employee; and open your heart to receive the gifts that each of these roles present to you. Know that you cannot be defined by your roles, but you can perform them all with beauty and grace.

Practice Forgiveness and Atonement

Not identifying with your roles allows you to clean up your river and be ready to die at any instant. Liberating yourself from the labels of *victim, provider, single mom,* and so on allows you to forgive others, absolve yourself for your actions, and atone.

So often people will take great pride in announcing that they've forgiven their mothers for being cold and unloving or their fathers for being too demanding, but they would never ask their parents to forgive *them* for their actions. Whenever my clients tell me that they've finally been able to forgive one of their parents, I ask them to go to that parent immediately and ask forgiveness for the hard time they've put their mother or father through. Only then do they sever the energetic cords that keep them bound to that person and that story.

As hard as it is to say "I forgive you" when you've been wronged, it's harder to say "I'm sorry. I hope you'll forgive me." Remember, forgiveness is not about blame and stories—it's about dropping the story in favor of the dream of loving and living in peace. You can forgive your ex-husband and choose to have no relationship with him, for instance, but you also have to be willing to give up the story you create in your mind every time you let yourself think about how he wronged you and you suffered. You bring that relationship back to life each time you play the movie in your head and re-create your anger, resentment, and sadness. Today is the perfect day for letting go of that story, forgiving once and for all, and leaving your karmic baggage behind.

Asking for forgiveness is a very difficult task because you open yourself up to getting drawn into another person's drama. Your former spouse's story of being the wronged lover may have a payoff for him, so he may not be willing to relinquish the victim role simply because you'd like to dream something more empowering.

When you ask for forgiveness unconditionally, keeping in mind that the other person's choice not to participate in a new dream has nothing to do with you, you can find the courage to say, "I'm sorry that I hurt your feelings and disappointed you," regardless of whether he or she chooses to reciprocate. It may be enormously difficult for you to let go of your desire to be told "I forgive you"; what's more, you might have difficulty forgiving yourself. At hummingbird, you'll remember that like everyone else, you're on a journey of spiritual discovery and will make mistakes along the way.

Western psychology tells us that in order to heal our emotional hurts we must forgive those who wronged us and be forgiven by those whom we have wronged. The problem with this strategy is that it keeps us locked into the stories of victims, rescuers, and perpetrators. That's why it's important to let go of any judgment and forgive all who were involved before making amends. That way, you let yourself off the hook for having authored such an unimaginative story. You excuse yourself for thinking, *How could I have married that idiot?* or *Why did I loan my daughter the car the night she got into her accident?* Then you say you're sorry and make amends with life—you atone. After all, your real debt is with the universe.

One way to atone is by helping someone else in need; when you do, your stories are no longer personal stories and your debts are no longer personal debts. You see how your actions harmed everyone, and you spot opportunities to help others and make up for your transgressions against life itself.

One evening in San Francisco, a friend and I were walking to our car, which was parked a few blocks away. We were approaching a homeless woman who was asleep under some pieces of cardboard when we saw a fellow several steps ahead of us place a bill in the woman's cup. A few seconds later, we saw two teenagers come and steal the money from the sleeping woman. I thought of giving chase to the kids, but my companion took me by the arm, and we placed a $10 bill inside the woman's jacket pocket instead. That evening, my friend paid back a debt to life and taught me a great lesson about giving freely to others.

When you sacrifice for another, the universe will observe your quiet act of atonement. You'll feel the weight of your guilt beginning to lift, because while saying "I'm sorry" feels good, actually making up for your harmful actions feels even better.

Yet true atonement must be done anonymously. As Jesus said, "Do not let your left hand know what your right hand is doing" (Matt. 6:1–4); in other words, as soon as you start thinking and talking about what a noble act you've committed, it starts serving your ego's story. Remain instead at a higher level of awareness, dreaming a world in which you don't need validation because experiencing forgiveness and love are enough.

Prepare for Your Departure Tonight

When you begin to identify with your soul and experience your connection to Spirit in all its many expressions, you'll find rising within you the courage to live as if you're ready to die at any moment. You won't be embarrassed, ashamed, or intimidated as you boldly act in alignment with your deepest held values. Your life will naturally unfold according to your intent, and with love, you'll say "Hello" and "Good-bye" to the people who come and go in your life. You'll be confident that even if those you care about won't participate at first in your new dream, you won't be alone. You'll feel certain that dreaming partners will appear and join you in co-creating a new reality . . . and they will.

In the following exercise, you'll indulge in speculating about how that new reality might unfold; by doing so, you'll open yourself up to the ingenious and magical ways that the universe employs to help you manifest your dream.

Exercise: Write Your Eulogy

It can be difficult to tell the story of what's happening in your life right now, or of how you experienced a significant event, without using the characters of victim, rescuer, and bully; but by now you know it's crucial to do so if you want to break out of the nightmare. Now it's time to tell your entire heroic story from the perspective of hummingbird. What has been your journey, from the moment you were born until today? Write the story as if you'd just died and this is the eulogy to be delivered at your funeral.

What memories of your life would you want the people you love to hold on to? Think about what you discovered and what you experienced—the events of your existence that help define who you are—but also remember the small moments that capture the image of you living the way you intended to.

How did you touch others? What love did you find, and what love did you bring to the world? What were your adventures? What did you explore, and what did you learn? What did you create? What did you enjoy? In times of change, challenge, loss, and tragedy, how did you practice beauty? What did you achieve?

Keep in mind that you are the storyteller, so you can frame the facts any way you choose. It doesn't matter what eulogy someone else might write for you—tell the story the way *you* wish it to be told, capturing the essence of who you are. If you're not happy with the dream you've lived, go back and rewrite it. Remember to describe the gifts and powers you acquired as a result of the disappointments and tragedies in your life and to frame your story as a hero's journey. Jot down your initiations, your rebirths and reinventions, and your triumphs. If you find yourself writing the eulogy that you wish were true today but you haven't yet made amends for what you've done, by all means do so right away.

When you've finished, draw upon your emotional courage and read your eulogy aloud to your parents, spouse, and children. By sharing what you've written, you're letting those you care most about know what is most important to you. This practice establishes your intent with others, and they can begin to support you in the kind of life journey they now know you'd like to dream into being.

Cultivate Gratitude

Being ready to die at any instant allows us to live fully and dream courageously, but it also has the hidden gift of nurturing the seeds of gratitude within us. When we stop rushing around, keeping ourselves busy and distracted, we start finding that we have the time to look at the larger picture of our lives and acknowledge our blessings. After being felled by a stomach flu, for instance, we often awaken the next morning with a deep appreciation for a simple piece of toast and our ability to sit comfortably on a chair. After experiencing a brush with death or hearing about a sudden tragedy—an earthquake, a bridge collapse, a fatal car wreck—we look at our partner or children or best friends and think, *How lucky I am to have them in my life! I ought to spend more time with them and tell them how much I care about them.*

Gratitude, the feeling that we're blessed, helps us to stop being enslaved to our to-do lists and remember why we came here: to love, to learn, to grow, to discover what we can do to participate in the unfolding work of art called creation. Feeling deep gratitude reminds us of what we most value and inspires us to stop procrastinating, awaken from the nightmare of frenetic but meaningless activity, and start truly living the way we want to live, with boldness and originality.

~~~~~

AFTERWORD

We all have the potential to dream a sacred and courageous dream, one that goes beyond serving our personal desires and brings beauty to the world. Together, we acknowledge our own contribution to the dream without being overly impressed by ourselves, for being a part of the greater dream holds so much more meaning. We savor the experience of dreaming in partnership with others—the people we love, the people we know only by sight, and the people we'll never have a chance to meet. We encourage them to join us in dreaming.

In Inka, Hopi, Tibetan, Mayan, and other aboriginal societies throughout the world, the elders carry on the tradition of gathering around a fire when the moon is full and dreaming of a world that they'd want their children's children to inherit. On that evening, they quietly arrive in the circle of dreamers, knowing that while what they have to offer is just a tiny piece of the larger puzzle, it's important that they show up with love and intent and participate in the dreaming process.

At serpent, they know they need only sit by the fire. At jaguar, they realize they must bring with them their love and curiosity. At hummingbird, they offer their contribution without comprehending how it fits in to the collective dream. At eagle, they see the larger picture before them and understand the totality of the dream without being able to express or define it. They feel immersed in love, connected to all. No longer experiencing "I" but the power and wonder of Spirit, they become the moon and the stars, the fire and the smoke, each other and themselves, no one and everyone.

They are the dreamers and the sacred dream . . . and it is this that I wish for each one of you.

ACKNOWLEDGMENTS

First, I'd like to thank my partner, Marcela Lobos, without whose love and support I would have never found the courage to take on this project. Thanks to you, I have learned to dream my life into being.

There are many persons who contributed to the birth of this book—above all I am grateful to my editors, Nancy Peske and Shannon Littrell, who shaped and sculpted this manuscript into life. And finally, I'd like to thank Reid Tracy, president and CEO of Hay House, for his vision of what this book could become; and my friend Dr. James Hamilton, for offering me his nurturing home in the Andes where I could finish editing the manuscript.

ABOUT THE AUTHOR

Alberto Villoldo, Ph.D., the author of numerous best-selling books, is a psychologist and medical anthropologist who has studied the spiritual practices of the Amazon and the Andes for more than 25 years. While at San Francisco State University, he founded the Biological Self-Regulation Laboratory to study how the mind creates psychosomatic health and disease.

Dr. Villoldo directs The Four Winds Society, where he instructs individuals throughout the world in the practice of energy medicine and soul retrieval. He has training centers in New England; California; the U.K.; the Netherlands; and Park City, Utah.

An avid skier, hiker, and mountaineer, he leads annual expeditions to the Amazon and the Andes to work with the wisdom teachers of the Americas.

Website: **www.thefourwinds.com**

∾∾∾

We hope you enjoyed this Hay House book.
If you'd like to receive our online catalog featuring additional information on
Hay House books and products, or if you'd like to find out more about the
Hay Foundation, please contact:

Hay House, Inc.
P.O. Box 5100
Carlsbad, CA 92018-5100

(760) 431-7695 or (800) 654-5126
(760) 431-6948 (fax) or (800) 650-5115 (fax)
www.hayhouse.com® • **www.hayfoundation.org**

∾∾∾

Published and distributed in Australia by:
Hay House Australia Pty. Ltd., 18/36 Ralph St., Alexandria NSW 2015
Phone: 612-9669-4299 • *Fax:* 612-9669-4144 • www.hayhouse.com.au

Published and distributed in the United Kingdom by:
Hay House UK, Ltd., Astley House, 33 Notting Hill Gate, London W11 3JQ
Phone: 44-20-3675-2450 • *Fax:* 44-20-3675-2451 • www.hayhouse.co.uk

Published and distributed in the Republic of South Africa by:
Hay House SA (Pty), Ltd., P.O. Box 990, Witkoppen 2068
info@hayhouse.co.za • www.hayhouse.co.za

Published in India by: Hay House Publishers India,
Muskaan Complex, Plot No. 3, B-2, Vasant Kunj, New Delhi 110 070
Phone: 91-11-4176-1620 • *Fax:* 91-11-4176-1630 • www.hayhouse.co.in

Distributed in Canada by:
Raincoast Books, 2440 Viking Way, Richmond, B.C. V6V 1N2 •
Phone: 1-800-663-5714 • Fax: 1-800-565-3770 • www.raincoast.com

∾∾∾

Take Your Soul on a Vacation

Visit **www.HealYourLife.com®** to regroup, recharge, and reconnect
with your own magnificence. Featuring blogs, mind-body-spirit news,
and life-changing wisdom from Louise Hay and friends.

Visit **www.HealYourLife.com** today

CPSIA information can be obtained
at www.ICGtesting.com
Printed in the USA
FSOW01n1912180317
32003FS